PRAISE FOR *I'M POSSIBLE*

"Coming out of a long life of familial human trafficking, and believing that I am just a story with shattered pieces and all the ugly truths that come from living that life, I made the decision to end my life in 2016. Jeremy's story saved me moments before I was about to meet my demise. I thank God for the *I'm Possible* story and Jeremy every day. This book is another reminder that we all have struggles and overcoming them is possible!"

—Saoirse

"Jeremy is not normal—his gift allows him to capture stories of beauty and hope and redemption in ways normal people typically overlook. This is a guy who had to look fear in the face to get to where he's at today, and his story will inspire you to do the same. Plain and simple: the world is a better place because of Jeremy and his work. Once you read this book, you'll understand why."

—Chip Gaines

"This is a dangerous book if there's a dream you've been running from that feels too big. The stories inside will call you to the edge of a new adventure, just beyond the border of what you think is possible. Bravo, Jeremy Cowart. Thanks for a dare we all need to hear."

—Jon Acuff
New York Times bestselling author of *Finish: Give Yourself the Gift of Done*

"In the greatest stories, the hero finds a meaningful life by serving others. Jeremy Cowart has lived a meaningful life and shows us a path to do the same. This is a wonderful book by a wonderful man."

—Donald Miller
Author of *Building a Storybrand*

"What a pleasure to be inspired by one of our generation's great humanitarians with a creative genius."

—Gabe and Rebekah Lyons
Authors and founders of Q Ideas

"I've had the privilege of knowing Jeremy for many years now. There is no doubt he is an incredibly gifted artist. But what I admire most about Jeremy is that he is always thinking beyond what's just in front of him. He is a man of God-sized dreams. Sure, anyone can dream, but too many times we are crippled by the voices of fear and doubt. Few actually take the steps of faith to make what seems impossible a reality. You will be inspired to read of such a faith in Jeremy's story, *I'm Possible*."

–Chris Tomlin
Music artist and author

"If you crave a life of meaning, pick up *I'm Possible*. With his own artistic journey as the backdrop, Jeremy Cowart will lead you find your purpose, harness your gifts, and impact the world."

–Michael Hyatt
New York Times bestselling author

"Henry Ford once said, 'Whether you think you can or can't, you're right.' Jeremy Cowart has spent a lifetime believing that he can—even when it didn't make sense. His story will inspire you and remind you that you can do more than you ever thought possible."

–Dave Ramsey
Bestselling author and nationally syndicated radio show host

"Jeremy's story is a great reminder for all of us that every turn in our lives matters, every dream is meant to walk us toward another, and every person we come across has purpose."

–Annie F. Downs
Bestselling author of *100 Days to Brave* and *Remember God*

"Jeremy has a gift to see the depth of humanity and therefore create pieces, projects, and movements that the human soul deeply needs. I've always been inspired by him to dig deeper to make my 'art' a bit more unique and spiritually inspired."

–Caitlin Crosby Benward
Founder of The Giving Keys and songwriter

"Jeremy Cowart is the most creative person I have ever met. He sees the world differently from the rest of us. But Jeremy is much more than a dreamer or an idea guy. He also possesses the rare tenacity to overcome resistance to bring these dreams to life. When we spend time together, I always come away inspired. *I'm Possible* is not just his remarkable story; it's like sitting with Jeremy and letting him fill your heart with belief for your dreams too."

–Darren Whitehead
Pastor of Church of the City and coauthor of *Holy Roar*

"Jeremy is a longtime friend of mine, and he's painted a beautiful and engaging book using words instead of oils. What you'll find in these pages is a load of honesty and authenticity. What you will take away from this book is a desire to get out your own canvas, fill it with the kind of grace-filled observations Jeremy has written about, and lead a more engaged life."

–Bob Goff
Author of *New York Times* bestsellers *Love Does* and *Everybody Always*

I'M
POSSIBLE

I'M POSSIBLE

Jumping into Fear and Discovering
a Life of Purpose

JEREMY COWART

W PUBLISHING GROUP

AN IMPRINT OF THOMAS NELSON

Published in Nashville, Tennessee, by W Publishing, an imprint of Thomas Nelson.

Author is represented by the literary agency of The Fedd Agency, Inc., P.O. Box 341973, Austin, Texas 78734.

Insert page design and photos by Jeremy Cowart.

Thomas Nelson titles may be purchased in bulk for educational, business, fund-raising, or sales promotional use. For information, please e-mail SpecialMarkets@ThomasNelson.com.

Any Internet addresses, phone numbers, or company or product information printed in this book are offered as a resource and are not intended in any way to be or to imply an endorsement by Thomas Nelson, nor does Thomas Nelson vouch for the existence, content, or services of these sites, phone numbers, companies, or products beyond the life of this book.

Scripture quotations are taken from the Holy Bible, New International Version®, NIV®. Copyright © 1973, 1978, 1984, 2011 by Biblica, Inc.™ Used by permission of Zondervan. All rights reserved worldwide. www.zondervan.com. The "NIV" and "New International Version" are trademarks registered in the United States Patent and Trademark Office by Biblica, Inc.™

ISBN 978-0-7852-2377-1 (eBook)
ISBN 978-0-7852-2374-0 (HC)

Library of Congress Cataloging-in-Publication Data

Library of Congress Control Number: 2018915208

Printed in the United States of America

19 20 21 22 23 LSC 10 9 8 7 6 5 4 3 2 1

CONTENTS

CONTENTS

PART 4: PORTRAIT OF AN ARTIST AS A DREAMER

INTRODUCTION

Learn how to see. Realize that everything
connects to everything else.

—ATTRIBUTED TO LEONARDO DA VINCI

I'm prone to artistic obsession. I obsess over certain films, certain
artists, the motion of certain athletes, the music of certain musicians. And among my musical obsessions, Thom Yorke, the front
man for the alt-rock band Radiohead, ranks near the top. In fact,
you're reading this book because of him.

On a slow afternoon, I searched Google Images for a photo of
the rocker to use in a mixed-media piece of art. I found the perfect
image, a photo of Yorke staring straight down the barrel of a camera. Hair cropped. Beard short. The whiff of a smile. It was perfect
in its simplicity.

I downloaded the image, threw on my favorite Radiohead
album, and got to work. And just for kicks, I decided to capture
the entire process on a time-lapse video using both a cell phone
recording and the screen capture feature of my monitor.

I pencil-sketched the photo on a piece of paper, glancing at the monitor as I worked. I went over the pencil marks with a charcoal stick, using short and wispy strokes. I tossed the pencil sketch to the side, grabbed another sheet of paper, and redrew it again using blue oil pastels. I drew it again in red pastels. A third time in green. I scanned the four stand-alone drawings of Yorke into my computer, then imported them into Photoshop and layered them one on top of the other. I created a fifth layer, using a touch screen to draw over Thom's face with my finger. Another layer, another finger painting. Another layer, another finger sketch. Repeat, repeat, repeat.

I went back to the well, opened Google, and downloaded more images. Different-colored backgrounds. Textures. Shades and shadows. I combined the layers. Blurred. Sharpened. Smudged. Filled. I lost myself in creation, in the music. And when the music stopped, when the silence sucked me back into the room, I stepped back and looked at the modern, abstract, multicolored portrait of Thom Yorke I had created. It was unlike anything I'd ever seen.

A few weeks passed, and I kept coming back to that piece. There'd been something magical in the process, in losing myself in the wormhole of the Yorke portrait.

Should I make another run at a similar piece?

Easter is coming up.

Maybe I should do a portrait of Christ.

As soon as the thought hit, I set out to replicate the process.

I didn't start with an internet image this time though. Instead, I reached for my oil pastels and drew variations of Jesus from my imagination. I scanned the drawings, then incorporated a handful of images from my own photo library into the background. Christ's shoulders were covered with a flannel shirt from a homeless man I'd recently met. I cloned an eye from a man I'd met in Africa, cloned another from a blond-haired, blue-eyed model. I combined fragments of different beards from different headshots I'd taken over the years. I cut a Burger King crown from a photo I'd taken of a kid at my mom's school and placed it on Christ's head. He was coming together, this portrait of shared humanity, this everyman. It was a Christ collage, the culmination of years of work.

I recorded myself creating this image of Christ, and after watching it a half dozen times from beginning to end, after comparing it to the Thom Yorke production, I uploaded both to the internet—because why not? It didn't take long for the videos to garner a little attention, and within a few days the promoter of a Christian conference, Catalyst, called and asked if I could perform a live variation of that process at one of their upcoming events. Was it possible? I didn't know, but I'd try.

The day of the event came, and I walked the conference space, gathering artistic inspiration. I made my way through the crowd, shot photos of speakers and attendees, and uploaded them to my computer. I pulled textures and sketched on sheets of paper, then scanned it all into Photoshop. I combined those elements to create a mixed-media piece, a collage of people from the conference with the phrase "Be Present" over the top. I recorded myself doing all this, then played the video in front of the crowd of thirteen thousand people at the end of the conference. It turned out to be one of my favorite experiments in on-the-spot creativity, and it came out better than I could have imagined.

A few months later, I received a phone call from my friend Jon Acuff. He'd seen my work, and he wondered whether I'd share my story at his upcoming Start conference for creative entrepreneurs. Flattered, I agreed. But after we hung up, I replayed the conversation, and a weight set in.

Wait.

My story?

Who cares about that?

I've never had any trauma, though I guess I struggled with learning growing up.

I suppose no one quite knew whether I'd make it out in the real world.

Will that story resonate?

Maybe folks will listen if I put an artsy spin on it.

I checked out the conference website, considered their themes: ideas, dreams, action. These were the themes of my life, the natural tendencies I followed even when my parents, teachers, and mentors cautioned me that I couldn't pay the bills with art. How had I made it through? Why had I kept going? How had ideas, dreams, and actions manifested through all the seasons of my life?

I replayed my life, remembering those early years in school, where my average intelligence and short attention span had caused so many problems. Art and creativity had provided such an escape for me. I laughed as I recalled my trepidation about computers and digital cameras and Photoshop. I considered the people God placed in my life to encourage me to follow my ideas, my creativity. I made a note of the projects I'd done over the years—how they'd all started as seeds of ideas, how so many had grown taller than I'd ever dreamed. I remembered the people, the stories, the impact. All of it had grown from the simplest encouragement, based on Philippians 4:13, my parents had given me when I was young: "You can do all things through Christ who strengthens you."

I should just tell my story exactly as it happened.

The story of a kid who didn't think he could do anything and then grew up to learn that he is possible despite his childhood beliefs.

Impossible became "I'm possible."

And if I'm possible, everyone's possible.

With that I knew exactly what I'd share, and I knew how I'd do it too. I'd create a new presentation, one with the same feel of my Thom Yorke and Christ portrait videos. I'd use the same media—drawings, photographs, Photoshop—and I'd create a video. But instead of a simple recording of myself making a single art piece, the video would be more of a sequential short film with autobiographical vignettes, custom illustrations, personal photos, hand-drawn fonts that scribbled across the screen, clips from home videos, and behind-the-scenes footage from projects—all mashed up. It would be a film that shared how idea led to idea led to idea. How following creative dreams led to incredible possibilities.

For three days straight, I sorted through the fossils of my past and wrote, drew, scanned, compiled, recorded, edited, copied, pasted, erased, and revised. I managed to whittle the story of my life down to thirty minutes, a compilation of the most significant times, projects, and people in my life. As I produced the video portion of the presentation, I imagined the script. I'd start in Hendersonville, Tennessee, and tell how I'd struggled in school, discovered art, received lackluster results from aptitude tests, and gotten my first Mac computer. I'd share how art had led me to graphic design and how graphic design had led me to photography. I'd show photos of celebrities I'd made, but I'd show the photos of my humanitarian work too. I'd tell the stories of those I'd met in Haiti, Uganda, Rwanda, and Gatlinburg as well as stories of the friends I'd made through Help-Portrait. I'd be honest about failure and loss along the way, too, and I'd share how all those ideas, all those failures, all those experiences had led me to the most amazing idea, an idea rich with possibility: The Purpose Hotel. And at the end of it all, I'd remind the audience that the very word *impossible* can be deconstructed to spell "I'm possible."

And that's exactly what I decided to title my talk: "I'm Possible."

On the day of the conference, I shared my life story as the video projected behind me. It felt good to share all the facets of my life—the doubt, the joys, the defeat, the triumphs, the lessons, the experiences. After the video ended, I asked the audience what they had been too afraid to try. What creative ideas or dreams had they failed to follow? Then I encouraged them to take the first step. To follow their ideas. To speak their dreams aloud. Because if I, the struggling student who couldn't help but chase every idea that came into my brain, could do everything that I'd done, imagine what they could do. Anything was possible.

I stepped off the stage, took a deep breath, and realized that everyone was standing, applauding. There wasn't a dry eye in the room. I'd touched on a truth, and we all knew it.

Anything is possible. Anything.

The video I created all those years ago still serves as a monument of sorts. It's a testimony to the fact that ideas and dreams are like a contagion. One leads to another, which leads to another, which leads to another. When we follow those ideas, those dreams, a world of possibilities opens up.

But following ideas and dreams can be a scary thing. Anxiety, lack of self-confidence, and the fear of failure too often keep us from following the first idea. If we don't push through those fears and anxieties, we'll never experience the rich possibilities God has for us. In fact, we'll create alternative timelines that rob the world of our unique contributions and us of a life fully lived.

This book tells a particular story: my story. It shows how following ideas and dreams led me to an idea full of purpose—a hotel with a humanitarian purpose, to be exact—and ultimately to a life lived in the fullness of possibility. This book isn't just a catalog of my experiences and a celebration of my ultimate dream. It's an invitation to inspiration, an encouragement for you to harness your own particular ideas and dreams and follow them into new worlds of possibilities.

Your dreams just might change the world if you only believe this truth: *I'm possible.*

Part 1

PORTRAIT OF A STRUGGLING ARTIST

Chapter 1

THE LOST BOY

A lot of parents will do anything for their
kids, except let them be themselves.

−BANKSY

Not long ago, my mom told me that when I was in the third grade, my school's guidance counselor called to say she was concerned about me because I didn't make eye contact and I talked with my head down.

This news surprised me for three reasons: One, that conversation happened more than thirty years ago, and my mother only recently decided to mention that the conversation took place. Two, I didn't know that my school had a guidance counselor. And three, I had always tried my best to stay off the radar of my teachers (and of the guidance counselor I didn't know I had). Until that conversation with my mom, I thought I'd succeeded.

Back then, in other words, school wasn't my thing—and for good reason. Stick a quiet kid with a loud mind in the middle of a classroom, ask him to sit still and focus—and guess what will happen. He's bound to feel like a mismatch. He's bound to avoid eye contact. His teachers are bound to think he's not too bright. His counselors are bound to call home.

It was the same every year, every grade. My classmates seemed to be perfectly content sitting at their desks, learning about multiplication or constellations or North American colonization, even raising their hands to ask questions or offering to read aloud, but I always felt two steps behind, always on the outside, trying my best to look in. And no matter what subject we were covering, a couple of minutes into any lesson, I'd be crawling out of my skin, staring out the window and itching to get outside.

Wouldn't that tree make the perfect spot for a tree house?
It would be awesome to throw my G.I. Joes from up there.
Maybe I could fly paper airplanes from the tree house too.
Can a G.I. Joe fly in a paper airplane?
I need to find some camouflage paper.

Day after day it was the same old story. Day after day I received papers with Cs and Ds written in red ink at the top. Day after day I'd be reminded of my mediocrity. And at the end of every day, I'd walk through the front doors of my house, defeated about all the things that had gone over my head, and I'd tell my parents, "I can't do this."

"You can do all things through Christ who strengthens you," my dad would respond. And though I knew he believed it—it was in the Bible, after all—I didn't.

In the third grade, I brought home a report card that included

4

an F or two, and I figured my parents would finally come to terms with the truth—I really couldn't do this. I finally had the proof that I wasn't smart enough, that I couldn't succeed. They didn't buy it though. Instead, they were quick to point out that my report card also had Bs and Cs, and they congratulated me with a bouquet of balloons. "You can do it," they said over and over.

Aside from the curse of academia, being raised in Hendersonville, Tennessee—once famous for being where Johnny Cash lived, but now famous for being where Taylor Swift went to high school—was idyllic. My upbringing was picturesque in both the scenic and the domestic sense. I was the youngest of three boys, and despite (or perhaps because of) the age-mandated pecking order, I did my best to keep up with my older brothers, Mike and Benji. I held my own, more or less. And sometimes I tried to prove myself by jumping first off the highest cliff into Old Hickory Lake, climbing the largest tree to scout the perfect spot for our fort, being the first to venture into the town's "haunted house" at Halloween (which is saying something, because in the 1980s people could jump out and grab you without the fear of lawsuits), or sticking my head inside the hollow of a big tree.

My brothers and I were a rambunctious trio, always getting into something, but my parents softened our edges through the introduction of music. I guess my dad sensed some natural talent in the three of us. Using a few of his connections in the Christian music industry, he got us into a kids' group that sang backup when musicians needed children's vocals for their albums. And so, for close to ten years, we'd often make the thirty-minute drive from Hendersonville into Nashville to sing backup for artists like John Denver, Willie Nelson, Alabama, Sandi Patty, Amy Grant, Wayne

Watson, and Michael W. Smith. I built a solid discography as a backup singer, but that career tanked when I hit puberty and no longer sang like a soprano.

We spent much of our childhood in those music studios. After we finished our parts, we'd make our way back to the lobby, where we'd wait for Mom to pick us up. While we were waiting, I'd often look out the big glass doors to the street and lose myself in the questions that bombarded my mind.

Do those tourists wish they were musicians?

Did those homeless people have moms who picked them up from activities when they were little?

Should I give them some of the money I just made from singing backup?

Would they want to come to our church on Sunday?

Maybe we should get some homeless kids to join our group.

"Earth to Jeremy," one of my brothers would say, claiming it was the third time. In the car they'd tell Mom that I'd drifted off again, that I'd been daydreaming. She'd just smile into the rear-view mirror, never judgmental, and tell me it was okay to have an active mind.

My parents always encouraged us in the arts. At one point, sensing that I might have musical talent, they asked if I wanted to take piano lessons. I jumped at the chance, eager to play my favorite songs. So they signed me up, and I sat through a lesson. Then another. I made it through a month or two, but I still couldn't plink out the simplest songs in the book. Too much was going on in my head.

Fingers, keys, sheet music, foot pedals, turn page, mind the metronome, wrong finger, C sharp not B, turn page again. Overwhelmed doesn't begin to describe it. I was lost. I'd go home and tell my parents once again, "I can't do this."

"You can do all things through Christ who strengthens you," I'd hear back.

Still, I couldn't seem to escape mediocrity or outright failure, even at church. On Sundays I'd watch the other kids take notes and ask questions as I sat there with no clue as to what the pastor was talking about. On Wednesdays at youth group, we had to recite Scripture from memory, and all I wished was that the verse of choice would be Philippians 4:13 because, thanks to my dad, I knew that one by heart. It never was, though, so each week I hid in the back and avoided making eye contact with the youth minister when he called for volunteers. (As an aside, hiding was the one thing I was pretty good at.)

Even though doubts about my intelligence followed me there, church wasn't all bad. In fact, it offered me a consistent refuge. Not only was there the loving presence of God; there was also good-for-the-soul worship music, all my friends, and above all, the basketball hoop. I played basketball in the church gym for hours on end, just a skinny white kid trying to emulate Michael Jordan every day after school.

And while we're on the topic, now is as good a time as any to make this confession: I was obsessed with Michael Jordan as a kid. From the first time I saw him on television, I knew that man was art in motion. I watched as many games as possible, read every interview I could get my hands on, and mostly wore clothes with a Chicago Bulls logo. My room had red-and-black bedding, and the walls were covered with Michael Jordan posters. If you're a child of the eighties or nineties, you might expect that the famous

"Jumpman" poster was my favorite, and you would be right. I loved that poster so much, in fact, that my parents had a gold necklace made with the Jumpman silhouette embossed on it long before it became his personal brand logo. It hung around my neck every day. It was my prized possession.

I wasn't that great at basketball, however; I was just mediocre, which was pretty frustrating considering how much time I put into playing. And when I'd experience a particularly disheartening loss after a pickup game, I'd head home and say to my parents, "I can't do this." And just as you might suspect, my parents would correct me.

"You can do all things through Christ who strengthens you."

As I grew into adolescence, I kept walking down the road of "average"—average grades, average singing voice, average piano playing, average spiritual depth, and average basketball skills. It seemed I was average at most things until seventh grade. That's when everything changed.

I was enrolled in an elective art class, and we were assigned one of those projects every art teacher makes you do, a two-point perspective drawing using vanishing points. The teacher explained the concept, showed us an example—a road converging to a point on the horizon—and told us to create our own drawings. And before I had the chance to consider what two-point perspective I might create, an image came to me—a New York City street corner where two streets converged, the cityscape vanishing in the background. I set to work on it before the teacher even finished the lesson and didn't look up until the bell rang. Over the next two days, I was more focused than I'd ever been in any class, and when I finished the drawing, I brought it home to show my parents.

They just stared at it.

"Did you trace that?" my dad asked.

"No," I said.

My mom and dad looked at each other, then at me. They were speechless for a few moments. Then they proceeded to act like I'd won the World Series. They celebrated me, hugged me, said how amazing the drawing was. They wondered where I'd gotten that kind of talent—there weren't any visual artists in the family, not really. And as they celebrated my work, something like relief washed over me. Maybe I wouldn't be average after all. Maybe there was something I *could* do.

In art I'd tapped into something, a hidden, natural talent. And when I was making art, I had no problems focusing. I could pour myself into my work for hours, could become so lost in an idea that I'd lose track of time.

My parents saw my talent and passion, and they went all in to support it. For my birthday that year, they surprised me with what I still consider to be one of the best presents I've ever received. I walked into my bedroom, and there it was in all its glory—a black wooden drafting table with boxes of oil pastels and colored pencils sitting under a big bow. I sat down and started exploring all the art supplies. Within minutes I'd tuned out the rest of the world.

I spent countless hours at that desk, lost in colors, contours, light, and shadow. And I always felt content sitting still at that desk, the speed of my mind finally finding an outlet through my hands.

What if I add more of a shadow here?

Would this roof look more realistic if I added shingles?

Should I draw all the leaves a different shade of green?

I need to work on perfecting face asymmetry.

Should I base a drawing on one of my Michael Jordan posters?

I sank into my art, creating or revising in every spare moment. The year flew by, and before I knew it, my birthday had come back around. I went out with my parents on the night before my birthday, and when I returned home, I was met by a dozen or so people yelling "Surprise" in the living room. When the shock wore off, I noticed that everyone in the room was wearing the same T-shirt, emblazoned with a drawing of Michael Jordan—one of *my* drawings. My parents had printed my artwork on the shirts, and everyone wore them as proudly as if I were an actual artist worthy of mass production.

Though I managed to get by with average grades in most of my classes, by the time I entered high school, I found a place where things came easier. In art class I was an above-average student for the first time in my life. I had a gift. A knack. Mrs. Kandros—my art teacher for all four years—encouraged me and taught me as much as I could take in about geometric forms, contour drawings, color theory, simulating textures, watercolor and acrylic paint, ceramics, portraits, and abstract art. And I could take in a lot where art was concerned. In fact, I was a sponge. I comprehended and retained what she taught, then worked diligently to apply it to my craft.

If only every class in high school could be art. I'd be valedictorian.

Though I was showing promise in art, I continued to struggle with the never-ending mandatory classes, like biology, Spanish, geometry, literature, and world history. "I can't do this," I'd say after receiving a less-than-stellar grade on a test, worksheet, essay, or lab.

"You can do all things through Christ who strengthens you," my parents said. And now they had another way to encourage me. "You're really excelling in art," they'd point out.

My folks could have simply offered words, but they didn't. They heard my frustration and set out to help me understand just what might be possible for my life. Years before, my dad had taken Mike to a learning center to take a fancy aptitude test that assessed his strengths and weaknesses. The test had helped Mike gain clarity on the direction of his life, and my parents thought it might help me sort out my own as well. So we made our way to Atlanta, Georgia, and I spent two days completing the Johnson O'Connor Aptitude Assessment. It was a tiring process, and when it was over, I was sure I'd failed.

Weeks passed. The results came in. And the truth was, I *had* sort of failed. Here's a representative sampling of my scores:

Inductive Reasoning—15/100
Analytical Reasoning—5/100
Structural Visualization—15/100
English Vocabulary—5/100

And though you might be thinking this proves I really am a complete and total moron (which is what I thought at the time), consider my one high score:

Idea Flow—79/100

The test confirmed what we already knew: I was an idea guy, a creative. I was wired to be an artist. And as I looked around my room at the artwork that lined the walls, this became even clearer. Sketches of the Teenage Mutant Ninja Turtles, Michael Jordan, and my brothers' faces. Random comics I had redrawn to figure out how to make the cape look like it was moving in the wind or how to make the raindrops look reflective as they bounced off the getaway car. Different Bible verses I had hand-lettered in original fonts. And in the middle of it all was a canvas with a large painted arrow pointing up, with hundreds of tiny arrows going in every direction inside of it. The day after getting my results of the aptitude test, my parents had that canvas framed.

I suppose my story isn't unlike so many others—the story of an underwhelming, self-critical, self-conscious kid who believes he's anything but special. I wasn't good at the things other kids seemed to be good at. I lagged behind. And even when I discovered my propensity for art, even when I found something I excelled at, I still wasn't sure what to do with it. After all, was art all that useful?

My parents did what all good parents should do. They encouraged me all along the way, helped me stay in the game, kept reminding me of my value as a person. And when I discovered my natural talent for art, they supported me and cheered me on. They gave me the tools I needed to dream, to discover what might be possible.

After all, what is a dream but a vision of future possibility?

What is a dream but a culmination of ideas?

And what is a dream if not the best vision of what we can be?

We all have dreams, even if they aren't fully formed. It's the job of family, friends, and mentors (like Mrs. Kandros) to help us discover our dreams. And in some small way, maybe it's my job to help you discover yours. How? By reminding you of a few simple but profound truths.

You have potential, even if it's hidden.

You have talent, even if you're afraid to use it.

You can do all things, even if you don't believe it.

All these years later, I have four kids of my own, all with different temperaments, talents, and tolerances. Now I can see just how extraordinary my mom and dad were (and still are) with their fidgety, imaginative, expressive, impulsive, artistic son. They could have tried to sway my interests, to push me to be better in school, but they didn't. They knew the truth: I'd never change the world with math, science, or history, but I just might make a difference with art, creativity, and ideas.

And so, through the ups and downs of my younger years, my parents encouraged me to follow my creativity. They taught me the truth that shaped my life: *I'm possible; my dreams are too.*

But this isn't a singular, personal, Cowart-sized truth. It applies to you too.

You are possible; your dreams are too.

WHAT IS A
DREAM
IF NOT
THE BEST
VISION OF
WHAT WE
CAN BE?

Chapter 2

WHEN BEAUTY FOUND ME

Every child is born an artist. The problem is how
to remain an artist once he grows up.

—ATTRIBUTED TO PABLO PICASSO

Did you know that the human eye sees more shades of green than
any other color? That Leonardo da Vinci reportedly spent twelve
years painting *Mona Lisa*'s lips? That the world record for the wid-
est vocal range of any human is ten octaves? (Mariah Carey's range
is five octaves.) That English artist Andy Brown created a portrait
of Queen Elizabeth II by stitching together a thousand used tea
bags? That the longest-running show on Broadway is *The Phantom
of the Opera*? And that the small town depicted in Vincent van
Gogh's *The Starry Night* is Saint-Rémy-de-Provence in the south of

France, which is where he was staying as a patient in a psychiatric hospital when he painted it?

These were the types of super-useful things my brain retained in high school. Math formulas and grammar rules? Not so much.

By my senior year, I had taken every single fine arts class my school offered. During school I spent much of my class time and all of my free time at the end of one particular hall, the hall that housed all the art, drama, and chorus classrooms. That little corner of the school was my haven, the place where I knew I could achieve something beyond mediocrity. I was taking musical theater, concert chorus, and every visual arts class they could throw at me. I played Tony in *West Side Story*, where my role *required* me to make out with Maria onstage—score!

But as hard as I fell for the girl playing Maria over the months we rehearsed that musical, I fell even harder for painting. The canvas suited me, and as I learned new techniques, as I explored different expressions of the medium, people began to take notice. And it wasn't just my parents, my friends, and Mrs. Kandros. The community began recognizing me too.

My senior year I won the high school art show for my painting of abstract heads. Not everyone understood the piece though. After I'd worked on it for months, my dad asked if it was a painting of Martians. "Sure," I said; then I told him that was the beauty of abstract art: you see what you want. I'm not sure he understood, but he hugged me and told me he was proud.

For years I'd thought I was subpar, mediocre. For years I'd dreaded walking through the doors of school, dreaded being called on or called out, dreaded the anxiety that washed over me in those moments. But thanks to my corner haven and the people in it, school somehow transformed into a tolerable experience. (It still hurts when I think about all the schools that don't have art programs and all the young Jeremys walking around without an expressive outlet.) In art and creativity, I found an area of competency, somewhere I could excel. And in that, I underwent a sort of transformation. For years I'd been shy and lacking self-confidence, but now I morphed into a slightly less shy and slightly more confident kid who jumped at the chance to get involved in different things.

I suppose I became a sort of living Hendersonville variety show.

I break-danced in my school's talent show to Prince's "Kiss."

I had a great time at parties, though I never once drank or smoked.

I was voted student body vice president. That's right; I was a young politician.

I was even named Mr. HHS—Mr. Hendersonville High School—which was shocking and humbling, but also a real confidence booster.

When my senior year came to an end, I took the typical American next step and enrolled in college. But I wouldn't be studying business or history or math or any of those subjects that gave me hives. Instead, I'd pour myself into art. Or so I assumed.

Middle Tennessee State University was the school for me, and I'd decided to pursue fine arts, particularly painting. Sure, Van Gogh sold very few—maybe as few as two—paintings while he was alive. Sure, Rembrandt declared bankruptcy and had to sell his wife's grave. But I was just young enough, just naive enough, to believe I was different. I believed I could make it as a gallery artist.

Enthusiastic as I was, my parents openly wondered whether

becoming a starving artist was the best career path for their son. So the summer before my first college semester, my mom came to my room, sat on the edge of my bed, and asked whether I'd considered other artistic avenues.

"What do you know about graphic design?" she asked. I had never heard of it.

She told me that I could use my artistic skills to design ads. If I could design ads, I could find employment at an ad agency. If I could find employment, I could make money. And if I could make money, I wouldn't have to be a starving artist. Plus, I could paint to my heart's content in my free time.

The conversation piqued my interest, and I asked how I could get into graphic design. Then she started talking about computers and something called Photoshop. This was 1995, when computer design was still relatively new to the average computer user. I have no idea how my mom had the foresight to see graphic design as a viable occupation. I suppose I come from a line of innovative thinkers.

At any rate, the minute she brought up the computers, the intimidation set in like a weight.

This whole thing is dependent on using a computer and learning a complicated program?

Nope, not a chance.

Computers are for smart people, for people who can focus.

"I can't do it," I said, and my mom left the room without a word. She didn't let it go that easily though. I suppose she believed in me too much.

A few weeks passed, and Mom hadn't dropped any more hints about graphic design or Photoshop. I was sitting at my desk, drawing, when she walked in, carrying a box. It was emblazoned with the Apple logo—my first Mac. I was surprised, grateful, and at the same time, utterly mortified.

I opened the box, turned it on. Scroll, swipe, click, close, resize, open, browse, menus, icons, *anxiety*. I wanted to give up even before I started, but I remembered my parents' familiar words: "You can do all things through Christ who strengthens you." And as I considered their faith in me, their confidence, their investment, I knew I had to try.

I made my way to MTSU with my Mac in tow, and reluctantly I enrolled in the graphic design program—even though I still hadn't opened Photoshop, which had been preloaded onto the Mac. I still thought that Photoshop was for smart people, not for average guys with a knack for painting. But midway through my first semester, sitting in a graphic design class, we closed our books and the professor gave us our first project: design an album cover.

It was the perfect assignment, an assignment that aligned with my interests. Not only was I in a band with my brothers—a Christian band with three-part harmony that we called Threefold Chord—and we could definitely use an album cover, but the project would force me to use my computer and experiment with Photoshop.

I didn't know the true extent of what Photoshop could do at that point, but I decided my cover design would be a sort of mixed-media project. I scanned in a photo of the band—Mike, Benji, and me—and then spent hours playing with Photoshop's toolbar, history palette, and undo commands before giving up. I'd wanted a semitransparent layer, and I couldn't quite sort out how to do it. So I closed the computer and went to Kinko's, a chain store that provided commercial printing and copy services. I put transparency paper over the photo, scanned it into my computer, and then figured out how to put fonts over the scan.

A week after we were given the assignment, we turned in our projects. There were twelve of us in the class, and the professor wanted us to see each other's work. He hung those covers on the wall, and that's when I knew I could do this graphic design thing. I hadn't exactly figured out the ins and outs of Photoshop while creating the project, and the program was still daunting to me, but as I looked at my work next to all the others, I sensed possibility.

Threefold Chord kept booking gigs—even at the Grand Ole Opry and Hard Rock Cafe—and I chose to believe it was because of my album cover (still do). But as time went on, it became clear that our hearts were elsewhere. Benji was moving in a different direction, headed toward full-time ministry. Mike had never loved the whole idea of practicing. And while I had the discipline and the desire to make something of the band, I also had less musical talent than either of them. I had more potential as an artist than I did as a musician, and didn't I owe it to myself to put all my energy into my art? What would happen if I went all in and embraced graphic design by jumping headfirst into Photoshop?

So the band called it quits, I poured myself into Photoshop, and here's what happened: I fell in love with the program. I started small. I scanned photos in and added halftone pattern overlays or black-and-white faux copy machine effects to hide the pixilation. I played with different text effects—drop shadows, semitransparency, overlapping, vertical alignment. I also started noticing typography everywhere I went, and I tried to replicate what I saw in my own creations. I'd doodle on my sketchpad, scan in the drawings to sharpen them up, and then add backgrounds, styles, and colors—so many colors.

Soon I was making files from scratch and creating photo composites—combining multiple photos into one. I used paint effects to create brushstrokes. I discovered smudge painting and paper texture. I started using keyboard shortcuts.

The more I messed around with Photoshop, the more I realized I didn't know about it. The more I didn't know about it, the more determined I was to find out. And the more I found out, the more thrilled and hooked I became.

It turned out that Photoshop was the coolest tool on the planet.

As the fear and intimidation faded, I discovered Photoshop wasn't just a program for smart people. It was for anybody! In fact, as far as Photoshop went, I was the smart kid in my graphic design class, and my classmates started asking me for help. I offered them tips and tricks. We began collaborating on projects together, helping each other bring our ideas to life. We sharpened each other.

During my sophomore year, I decided that taking a photography class would be a natural progression into this technological world I had unlocked. I had a Canon Rebel 35mm that my parents had bought me in high school—another one of their attempts to encourage my creativity—so I enrolled in a class. But I soon found out that a university-level photography class wasn't as simple as showing up and taking photos. For every hour shooting or developing, there were at least two hours of classroom lecture, and during those lectures, my professor might as well have been speaking in Greek—shutter speeds, apertures, ISO, technicalities—numbers, numbers, numbers. As I zoned out, all I could think about were the compositions that would make the best photos—the lights and shadows, the colors.

That class was a reminder: I didn't have what it took to be successful in the classroom. But to shake that nagging sense of failure, I busied myself with other things. I spent more time working on projects for other art classes. I hung out with my friends. I led worship at a local church. I fell in love.

That's right. I fell madly in love.

I was playing guitar and singing one Wednesday night at our local hang spot, and I spotted a girl. She was surrounded by other girls, none of whom I knew, and she was by far the most beautiful of the bunch. *What will happen if I run over right after I finish my set and introduce myself to her?*

She was gone before I could make the introduction, but I found out that her name was Shannon. And then I saw her again a couple of nights later at an intramural football game. Fate? I thought so. My heart quickened, and my stomach felt as if it were full of helium. I did my best to steady my nerves, walked across the field to where she was standing, and introduced myself.

I don't remember what I said, whether it was smooth or came out in a jumbled mess. I don't remember exactly what she said either. But I do remember that we spent hours together talking on that first night. We met the next night, then the next. I asked her to go to a local concert, "just as friends." She agreed.

At that concert, we sat together and talked some, but between sets we mingled around the room too. Once, she excused herself from the table and made her way to the back of the room, where she talked with a woman in a wheelchair. She was making conversation with someone who'd been alone.

This girl's different.

This girl's amazing.

I have to really ask her out—not just as friends.

Being the extremely classy guy that I was (and still am), our first official date consisted of running errands and going to Walmart. At the end of that most romantic evening, I asked her out a second time, and for whatever reason, she agreed. I was broke in those days, so our second date consisted of driving around town while I shot photos for a class assignment. She was my model and my new favorite subject to shoot, and between shots she told me about her life, how she'd been raised by the best parents, how she loved God, how she was always drawn to people who were alone or hurting or in the margins.

Where has this girl been all my life?

I didn't waste any time, and two weeks later I told her I loved her. She was driving away in her car with the window rolled down, and her face lit up as she said, "I know."

The good news that semester was that I didn't scare Shannon off with my proclamation of love so early in our relationship. The bad news was that I got a D in my photography class, and I suspect the only reason I didn't get an F was that I'd found the best model on campus. I burned with insecurity, felt the hopelessness of utter inadequacy. (Cue flashbacks to grade school.) But Shannon offset the discouragement of that low grade with her encouragement. "A grade doesn't determine your worth," she said, and though it was still early in our relationship, she said she'd stick it out with me no matter what grades I made. Turned out she loved me, too, with the sort of unconditional, faith-giving, confidence-boosting love my parents had shown me all those years.

Despite Shannon's encouragement, I believed photography wasn't for me, so I decided two things: One, I was going to quit photography and stick to graphic design. Two, I was going to do everything in my power to get Shannon to marry me. After all, girls with that capacity for love didn't come around every day.

That photography class reinforced bad belief, a standardized way of thinking. I believed that getting an A meant I was great, a B or C meant I was okay, and a D or F meant I sucked and that I couldn't do something. I believed that if I couldn't succeed in the classroom, I couldn't succeed at all. I had assessed my whole life by that grading system, judged myself according to a state-mandated curriculum—a judgment that couldn't have been more inaccurate. If I had gone on with that way of thinking, if I hadn't overcome the fear of photography, my possibilities would have been limited. Significantly.

I wasn't ready to hear it, but even then, Shannon knew I was more than that D in photography. She knew I could do anything I put my mind to creatively, and she quietly set out to support my art, no matter what the medium. Looking back, I can see now how she never hesitated to support me in my creative journey. She was prepared to follow me into it, and she never again mentioned that barely passing grade, not even when I decided to pursue photography as a full-time job.

I made good on both post-photography-class decisions: I didn't take another photography class, and I poured myself into graphic design, continuing to excel in it. I also asked Shannon to marry me during my senior year of college. She said yes, and in August 1999, she walked the aisle of First Baptist Church in Hendersonville, Tennessee, while I sang "The Other Side of Me" by Michael W. Smith. (It was cheesy, sure, but it was the nineties.) We began our life together, and as we settled into new lives and new careers, I avoided photography at all costs. In fact, I wouldn't pick up another camera for years, not until it became professionally necessary. And even when I did return to photography, I never dreamed I'd become a professional photographer, one of the most influential in the industry at that. And I can trace my success in photography to one person—Shannon.

If you're anything like me, you're your own worst critic. You take in the lies the world feeds you: *You can't do it. It's too hard. You're a failure.* Even worse, you allow those lies to limit your possibilities and cap your dreams. The truth is, that's exactly what I would have done if it hadn't been for Shannon. Without her encouragement I would have believed I was a failure. Without her support I would've stuck with graphic design and never made the leap to photography in 2005. If it hadn't been for her affirmation, I wouldn't have pursued my ultimate dream, a dream filled with so much purpose.

True love—the godly love of a spouse, family member, or friend—pushes back the lies and reminds you of the truth. It tells you you're possible, that your ideas and dreams matter. And that's why it's important to surround yourself with the right people— people who love you, believe in you, and are willing to walk into your dreams with you. Without people like that, the lies of mediocrity or failure seem more resonant, louder. Without them, fear becomes crippling. Without them, dreams and possibilities are limited. But with them, all things are possible.

I thank God every day for the love of a good woman. I thank God that He's given me Shannon to encourage me and to speak the truth over my dreams—even if the truth is that a particular idea of mine isn't fantastic or a project isn't worth pursuing or I'm a touch overconfident in the moment. Without Shannon I wouldn't have pushed back the lies and discovered my true path. Without her I'd have settled for the merely good instead of reaching for the more incredible possibilities.

SURROUND
YOURSELF
WITH THE
RIGHT PEOPLE—
PEOPLE WHO
LOVE YOU,
BELIEVE IN YOU,
AND ARE WILLING
TO WALK INTO
YOUR DREAMS
WITH YOU.

Chapter 3

BIRDS OF A FEATHER

Great minds discuss ideas. Average minds discuss events. Small minds discuss people.

–ANONYMOUS

I designed a restaurant menu for my senior design thesis, and to this day I consider it as close to a work of art as any restaurant menu can be. That said, I tweaked and tinkered with it up to the last minute. In fact, I tweaked it *past* the last minute and handed the project in late. Professor Buxkamper, who had turned out to be one of my favorite professors, handed down a passing grade, but it came with some advice: "Your biggest problem is you can't finish. You're always trying to make it better. You need to learn how to make deadlines."

He was right, of course. He'd identified the pattern throughout my four years with him, and now my need for perfection had bitten me in the artistic rear. But though his was valuable advice, I wondered if any creative who believed something was completely finished and finally perfect could be trusted.

I graduated and began an internship at a graphic design and marketing firm in Nashville. I'd learned the ins and outs of Photoshop at MTSU, and I was ready to put my skills to the test. I would apply what I'd learned at college in a real-world setting as I worked on illustrations, branding, packaging, and logos. It was the opportunity I'd been waiting for, a stepping-stone on my path to breaking into the advertising world.

I walked through the glass doors on my first day, imagining the kinds of things I'd design—a new Coca-Cola campaign, print work for Apple, the next Nike Swoosh. The possibilities were endless.

Sweet, young, naive Jeremy.

The work wasn't nearly as sexy as I had expected. I worked on packaging for mom-and-pop shops, accounting firms, law offices. I pulled together a few small banner ads for a publishing company. I did whatever work came across my desk. And then, almost without warning, my internship transitioned into full-time employment. The transition was so fast, in fact, that I didn't have time to say no. Not that I would have. Wasn't this what adulthood was all about? Saying yes to the right opportunity. Clocking in. Doing grunt work. Having unreasonable turnaround times. Shelving your great ideas for the day you make partner, the day you have the corner office, the day you arrive.

The internet was in its infancy in those days, but at the firm we had unlimited access. I was becoming skilled at surfing the web during downtime, and, knowing I understood this new technology, my boss asked whether I'd help out with some web design for a client. I jumped at the chance. I could visualize the ads and knew how the users would react to them. But as I pushed into the project, it turned out I was just a workhorse, not an idea generator. My vision didn't matter. Zero creativity was required. In fact, very little technical ability was required. My excitement flattened. And yet the boss loved my work.

"You've got a good eye for this web stuff," he said. "Do you want to move to our web division?"

I didn't know I could show such potential just by resizing a few ads, but sure, okay, I was game to try something new. And who knew? Maybe they'd even let me sit in on a brainstorming session for a client website. Maybe they'd let me give a little creative direction. (Spoiler: they didn't.)

I was thrust into the new world of HTML, CSS, and JavaScript, and I had to learn it all. With all these changes, though, two things didn't change—the pace at which I was asked to produce and the lack of creativity involved in the work. As the days wore on, I found myself in a maddening rhythm: clock in, learn a new computer language, resize ad, swap photo, replace font, make frame border invisible, clock out.

As frustrating as this was to me, there was an upside. I met a guy named Jeremy Pinnix, who ran the web division, and we became fast friends, which was sort of a surprising development considering we didn't have too much in common. Pinnix was older than I was, definitely more focused, extremely book smart, and able to retain anything anyone said to him. Being around him made me feel better—sharper, inspired, more balanced. And because of my growing relationship with Pinnix, I didn't dread going to work nearly as much as I had before I moved to the web division.

Even Pinnix couldn't fix my lack of passion for the work, though, and after a year I suppose my lack of enthusiasm started to show. I was a little too slow to meet my deadlines, a little too blasé about the content. At any rate, one Friday our boss called me into the office and fired me. He even suggested that I might want to consider finding another career altogether.

"Jeremy, maybe you should consider a career in youth ministry."

Ouch. That's harsh. (There's nothing wrong with youth ministry, of course, but I took his comment as an insult.)

I drove home that day with a box of stuff from my office desk sitting on the passenger seat, feeling deflated but not defeated. The familiar words of my parents echoed in my memory: *You can do all things through Christ who strengthens you.* Bolstered by their words, by their unfailing belief, I didn't allow myself to get down in the dumps. I considered the tools I'd picked up at school and the ones I'd learned in that first job. I'd learned Photoshop. I knew design. I knew the web in a day and age when not too many knew the web. I could do anything I wanted to do, and what I wanted to do more than anything was create.

I was a little concerned about telling Shannon I'd lost my job. It was a failure more significant than my D in photography class, and I wondered whether she'd still support me, still believe in me. She knew the three-part plan I'd had even before taking that first job: one, land a job in the cool and sexy world of advertising; two, gain the respect of my peers and clients and make partner in the firm; and three, jump ship at the age of forty to become a freelance graphic designer. Now step two had come to a premature end. Would she be disappointed? Would she tell me we needed income, that I needed to bail on my dream and pursue something more practical?

Not my wife.

At home I delivered the bad news, and as if to prove she was my true soul mate, Shannon encouraged me. My dream wasn't dead, she said. She believed in me, she said. Everything was still possible.

It's a moment burned into my memory. As undeserving as I was (and continue to be), Shannon offered me the purest form of solidarity. She was with me through success and failure, for better or worse, and that "withness" set a precedent for our marriage. We would continue the journey together, and even when we stumbled, our commitment to each other would provide a safe place to land.

I hit the streets the very next day, started putting out feelers. Through my friend Geoff Alday, I found another job at a small graphic design company—Smoking Dog—that specialized in websites. In less than a week, I was back on track. There were only six of us in the office, and the smaller team allowed me to put my minimal coding skills to good use and let me flex my creative muscles.

Months into the gig, a client said he wanted a complicated and artistic graphic front and center on his website. The company handed the reins over to me, and as I considered the client's needs, I retreated to what my friends had come to call Jeremyland—that place where I tune out the world and get lost in ideas. I considered the options. Textures. Colors. Lines. More textures. The idea came together, and I set to work. Within twenty-four hours I'd created a fifty-layer Photoshop graphic that blew both my bosses and the client away. That was my first success at Smoking Dog, and as the partners asked me to do more complicated, more creative work, my confidence grew.

In my free time, I freelanced a little—you always need a side hustle—and landed a gig with a friend I knew from church, a small-business owner who ran an armoire shop. She needed a website redesign and asked if I could take all new photos of her merchandise to feature throughout the new site. "But I got a D in photography class," I wanted to tell her. Instead, I swallowed my hesitation and said yes, convinced I could pull it off. I spent a day snapping shots of furniture, and when I developed the film and presented the photos to the client, she was over the moon.

Well, look at that. I apparently have an eye for armoires.

The successes kept coming. My portfolio grew. Calls started rolling in. One of those calls was from a high-end advertising agency in Nashville, and they were inquiring about an opening in their web division. Would I be interested? It was a new challenge, maybe a sign that my life plan was back on track. At their request I sent my portfolio to the company, made my way through the interview process, and sure enough, got the job. I showed up on my first day extremely pumped about all the big-name clients I'd be working with. But again, the big ad-agency world was something less than what I expected. My first assignment was a website redesign for an air-conditioning company, and in case you're wondering, it's impossible to make an AC unit look any sexier than an AC unit, no matter how many Photoshop layers you use. But boring as it was, monotonous even, I pushed into the work. I didn't want to get fired again.

Months in, though, things hadn't become any more exciting. I called my dad and told him all about the job, and he could tell just from the sound of my voice that it wasn't everything I'd hoped it would be. So he gave me his hard-fought wisdom. Everybody has to do work they don't like, he said. And he followed that up with the most deflating comment: "People rarely like what they do for a living, Jeremy."

Could it be true? I wondered. The prospect sounded really depressing, and I didn't want to spend eight hours a day for the rest of my life doing something that sucked. I wanted to buck the system, go against the grain. I wanted to do something that energized me.

As I got to know my new coworkers, I began to see a trend in their conversation, and it made me wonder if my dad was right. They complained about everything. They weren't paid enough. They were overwhelmed. Management was terrible. Deadlines were tight. Day after day, their grievances made the air feel so heavy.

Perhaps because of my dad's comment, I started noticing a similar heaviness outside of work too. Every week I hung out with a small group of guys, and we'd talk about life and discuss books or movies or whatever. But the longer we hung out, the more our talk seemed to turn to the countless things that were wrong with life: "I hate my job." "I hate where I live." "My boss sucks." "You'll never believe what so-and-so did." "Life is such a drag." Instead of lifting each other toward the light, it seemed we were keeping each other mired in the darker aspects of life.

Surely we had better things to talk about than how scorned or bored or disappointed or misused we felt. *Don't we have dreams to chase and seeds to sow? What do we want our lives to look like? Shouldn't we be helping each other get there?*

I couldn't get it out of my head, this desire to motivate instead of suffocate. And as I carried that desire into work, it became downright overwhelming. My fellow creatives wasted so much energy on negativity. Was there a way I could flip the script, help turn the negative into positive? I thought of all the incredible things we could create together if only we had a more positive, more intentional environment.

Desperate for an outlet, a more positive space, I drafted an e-mail to ten friends in Nashville who were web or graphic designers like me. How would they feel about forming a loosely connected group that would support and encourage one another in our craft? We could e-mail back and forth to spitball ideas, ask questions, and share resources and insights. We could brainstorm ways to turn the mundane into something imaginative, both in our work and in the world around us. We could elevate the conversation, encourage one another to chase ideas, and create joy instead of dwelling in discontentment. And then, right before I pushed Send, I named the group after Nashville's area code—"the 615."

The response was immediate and enthusiastic. It was proof that people really did crave optimism and belonging, and proof that I invented social media. (I kid, I kid.) The group steadily grew, both in size and in purpose. We referred each other for projects and showed new members just how inclusive and collaborative the creative process could be. We had dinner meetups and went on camping trips. We became more than just a support to each other; we became a real community. We were advocates and dreamers and doers, and all of it was so life-giving.

Over the next several years, the 615 continued to build each other up, and by the time I left the group to transition into photography full-time, it had more than two hundred members. Two hundred members committed to chasing imagination, creativity, and collaboration. Members who weren't content to dwell in discontentment, who weren't content to talk about people or events.

Members who wanted to shape ideas.

Ideas, ideas, ideas—I *love* ideas.

The saying "Great minds discuss ideas; average minds discuss events; small minds discuss people" has been attributed to a lot of people, including several famous ones (like Eleanor Roosevelt). But when I consider that quote, I often think about the 615, about how so many of us were idea driven and how we encouraged one another to chase down those ideas and put them into action. That group provided a source of encouragement and positive light in a time when I was surrounded by folks who seemed to trade creativity for complaint.

All of us need encouragement. All of us need the positive light of positive people, especially when we're creating new things or exploring and implementing our ideas. In fact, the quality of our creative community can be the single most important factor in determining whether we become better or bitter. Finding people who are steadfast and uplifting turns us into the best versions of ourselves, and the 615 was nothing if not steadfast and uplifting. Over the years they've encouraged and backed my ideas. They've pushed me to refine my processes, jump into challenges, and chase audacious dreams. I hope I've done the same for them.

As a photographer, I've come to understand that we're all a little like a photograph. Just as a photograph is composed of different sources of light, both positive and negative, so are we. Early in my career, I realized that although I was surrounded by people I loved and admired (including many who are still in my life to this day), some of those folks weren't positive sources of light. In fact, their "negative fill" was affecting my heart. To keep it in photography terms, it was interfering with my "sensor."

As I came into that understanding, I began to distance myself, sometimes on purpose but often unintentionally, from those shadowy sources. Some of them picked up on that distance. In fact, one of my friends confronted me about it.

"Jeremy, you don't want to hang with us anymore. You hang around only cool and important people."

His comment felt stark and almost unfair. Sure, my career had taken me down a path of connection to others outside of my normal circle, but as I considered his comment, I realized he couldn't be more wrong. It wasn't that I wanted to be around only cool or important or interesting people; it was that I wanted to spend time with more positive sources of light. I wanted to be with folks who tackled problems with collaborative, creative positivity. I wanted to work with dreamers, with people who discussed ideas about how to make the world better, and it just so happened that a few of those people happened to be well-known.

Creativity, technical proficiency, ideas—you can hone them to death, but they'll take you only so far. Without surrounding yourself with the positive light of good community—whether family, friends, or coworkers—you'll never achieve your full potential. Without positive light, your possibilities will be limited by fear or self-doubt or defeatism. And that poses the question: Are you surrounding yourself with positive light or negative? Are you in community with people who lift you up or drag you down? And what about you—are you making people better or bitter?

If my story is anything, it's a testament to positive sources of light—sources like my parents, Shannon, and the 615. Had I not allowed them to encourage and pour into me, I would have never chased down my ideas, would have never allowed those ideas to become dreams, would have never turned those dreams into possibilities. Why? Because possibilities are only illuminated when they're exposed to the right kind of light.

THE QUALITY OF
OUR CREATIVE
COMMUNITY CAN
BE THE SINGLE
MOST IMPORTANT
FACTOR IN
DETERMINING
WHETHER WE
BECOME BETTER
OR BITTER.

Part 2

PORTRAIT OF A THRIVING ARTIST

Chapter 4

THE UNEXPECTED GRACE

Life offers you a thousand chances . . .
all you have to do is take one.

–FRANCES MAYES

In the early 2000s, I was still working at the high-end advertising agency, and while they were happy with my work, I was also carving out a vocational double life. I spent my nine-to-five in the office, but on the side I was growing a freelancing business. My side hustle was gaining steam because a few of my college buddies—Dave Barnes, Matt Wertz, and Brandon Heath—were trying to break into the music industry, and they'd asked me to design their album covers and websites. They passed my name on to other friends and friends of friends, and soon musicians such as Andy Davis and Bebo Norman started calling. That freelancing was my saving grace, because those projects were proving to be way more fulfilling than my desk job.

Clients kept calling. My side business kept growing. More and more, I wanted to leave my agency job and go out on my own, something the 615 and Shannon were both encouraging me to do. I wanted to set my own pay and my own deadlines, develop my own ideas. I wanted to work on projects that excited me, with people who inspired me. I wanted to have the freedom to do more.

Still, the doubts kept nagging.

I know I'm talented, but am I talented enough?

Why would I risk a consistent paycheck and health benefits for an unpredictable income?

I've always said I'd stay in advertising until I was forty, and then I'd start freelancing. Shouldn't I just stick with the plan?

If I fail, where will that leave me?

To make matters more complicated, Shannon and I had started talking about having children. Our expenses were bound to grow with the addition of a couple of kids, and didn't that mean I needed a secure job, one that provided a safety net? Wasn't that what rational adults did?

I decided to do the adult thing and stick it out at the agency. But then I walked into a coffee shop and saw Jimmy Abegg, and everything became more abstract—just like one of his paintings.

When I was growing up, my dad was a subscriber to a Christian music magazine—*CCM Magazine*—and I read it religiously. In fact, it was the only thing I read voluntarily in those days. It was a biweekly publication, so twice a month I'd hole up in my room and read interviews with contemporary Christian musicians like

Michael W. Smith or dc Talk or Jars of Clay or Sixpence None the Richer. I loved the interviews and the stories, but when the magazine arrived in the mailbox, the first thing I'd do was flip to the back, where the latest Jimmy Abegg painting of some artist was splashed across the page.

Abegg's style was abstract and loose, his color palette vivid. He created visual holes I fell into for hours. And when I found out he was also a musician, I started listening to the albums he played on, and I came to admire him even more. He was the kind of artist I could aspire to become, the kind who was making it up as he went along. So when I saw him at a coffee shop in Nashville in my early twenties, I was completely starstruck.

Jimmy was standing in line like a normal human, but still he held himself to the side, off-kilter, like some cubist character. How would I approach him, this artist I'd followed for all these years? And why was he different from the other artists I'd worked with—bigger, somehow able to occupy more space even though he was so thin? A cold sweat broke out on my forehead. My fingers tingled. Was I breathing?

I knew I might never get the chance to meet Jimmy Abegg again, so I gave myself a pep talk—*You can do this, Jeremy*—and I walked up to him.

"Hey, man." I extended my hand to shake his. "I'm a big fan of yours."

He smiled, shook my hand, and thanked me. Then he asked if I'd share his table.

Jimmy Abegg just asked me to have coffee with him?

After we got our coffees, I pulled out the chair across from him, and we struck up a conversation. After a few minutes, I told him

I'd love to send him some of my work. I wanted to get his opinion, maybe even hear his critique. He agreed, and we exchanged e-mails.

Jimmy Abegg gave me his e-mail address?

I sent him some portfolio samples—a couple of websites, some album covers, some pictures of my paintings—and he was kind enough to respond. He liked what he saw, and—get this—he asked if we could meet again. We set up a time. I shook with excitement.

We met in that same coffee shop, and he spoke so much life and encouragement into me. He shared some of his wisdom about art, the music industry, and the uphill climb that comes with the creative life. We talked about the agency world, the grind, the lack of creativity in commercial advertising. I told him about my dreams of becoming my own boss, of being more creative with my clients.

We talked through it all, and as we said our good-byes and stood to leave, Jimmy gave me his last two cents: "You should quit your job tomorrow and start your own business."

Did he just say I should quit my job? Tomorrow?

It was so nonchalant, so assured, as if he was saying, "You should open that window and look to see what's outside." And come to think of it, that was exactly what he was saying.

It struck me then how much I'd been missing the guidance of someone who understood the life I was leading because he was a little farther down the road in his creative journey. Shannon was a huge source of encouragement, and my 615 friends were quick to weigh in when I bounced something off them—both of which I relied on and valued. But it felt different to hear insights from someone who'd navigated the ups and downs of the creative life for years.

We set the date for another meeting, and I drove home. I walked through the door and told Shannon, "Jimmy said I should quit my job tomorrow."

She looked right at me with the same assuredness Jimmy had shown hours earlier and said, "Yeah, I'm for it. Quit your job tomorrow."

There was no hesitation in her voice. She didn't ask how we'd afford our lifestyle, how we'd manage the finances. She didn't raise concerns about security or savings or retirement or how she'd manage to quit her job as a physical therapist so she could stay home and raise kids. In fact, as if to reiterate her utter belief in our shared journey, she repeated: "Quit. Tomorrow. It's time to do your own thing."

That was all it took. Jimmy's belief in my ability to succeed and my wife's unwavering support killed the questions, killed the fear. The next day I went into the office and put in my two weeks' notice. And after that two weeks was up, without taking so much as a vacation day, I jumped headfirst into starting my first company—Pixelgrazer, a freelance graphic design company.

I let my connections in the music industry know I was open for business, and they spread the word. Calls came in. Work lined up. And the fact that I knew very little about running the day-to-day affairs of a company didn't keep me up at night nearly as much as the nonstop design ideas swirling around in my head. There was so much I wanted to create. But pulling it all off would require crazy technology and tons of back-end (coding) knowledge—knowledge I didn't have. Maybe I should have considered that minor detail before I made the leap.

I was almost asleep one night when the name came screaming

in—*Jeremy Pinnix.* It shook me awake, and I sat straight up in bed. Nothing in the world made more sense to me in that moment than to have my buddy from my first job become my business partner in Pixelgrazer. He was the most brilliant web developer I knew, and like me, he loved innovation as much as he hated office politics. Better yet, unlike me, he lived in both sides of his brain, right *and* left, and he'd know how to run a business.

I called him early the next morning, fully prepared to plead my case, but I didn't have to beg at all. I asked. He said yes. We hit the ground running.

Album covers, websites, merchandise—we did it all, and our little company was slammed in no time. The client base grew, and some of the biggest names in the pages of *CCM Magazine* started calling. A musical artist named Derek Webb reached out for some design work, and I stammered through the phone call, awestruck. Kevin Max hired us to create his website, which was a complete dream because not only had he always been my favorite member of the band dc Talk—I had long sensed that we were the same type of weird, and I was right—but also because he was as eager to think outside the box as I was. I poured myself into all my work but paid extra attention to the work for Derek Webb and Kevin Max, and that attention to detail paid off. Derek and Kevin passed my name along to some of their friends, and the noise Kevin Max's page made when it launched put our small design shop on the map.

There wasn't much Pixelgrazer didn't do and almost nothing we wouldn't try. *What have people not seen before? Can I have a black-and-white illustration at the bottom of a page with a color GIF at the top, and then merge the two just by scrolling? Can I create a transparency effect by removing every other pixel out of an image and then creating a layer underneath it so that when the user scrolls, the lower layer is visible?*

I spent hours designing interfaces in Photoshop and exporting hundreds of graphics for just one page; then I'd lob it over to Pinnix to see if it was doable, unreasonable, or impossible to code into the website. If it was even remotely possible, he'd build it. Innovation, creativity, and ideation led our process, and Pixelgrazer reaped the rewards.

Our musicians loved our work, and they referred us to their record labels. Michael W. Smith's label, Rocketown Records, hired us to create all their artist websites. Other, smaller labels followed suit. Some of the work we did required photos—images for websites, assets for albums, promo shots for print work. So out of necessity, I started shooting more and more, even though I was still unsteady with the camera, still unsure of myself. I mentioned as much one day over lunch with my personal Yoda, Jimmy Abegg.

"Have you considered this new thing called a digital camera?" he asked.

He might as well have been speaking Japanese, which I don't speak.

"You have to buy one," he said. "Canon just released the PowerShot G1. It takes 3.3-megapixel shots. You shoot, upload the image to your computer, import it into Photoshop, and you're ready to work."

Did he say I can just take a picture and it will transfer to my computer?

I considered my workflow. The majority of hours in my day were spent using Photoshop, and increasingly I was using my own photos in my designs. It took so much time and effort to shoot a photo, take it to the lab, wait for it to be processed, scan it into the computer, and import it into Photoshop. I considered the number of steps a digital camera could remove, the amount of time it could save, and my mind was blown. I went out the next day and bought one.

I unboxed the camera at the office and played with its dials and settings. One thing was clear: I had no idea how to use it. I had been scraping by with shooting for clients, but if Pixelgrazer wanted to deliver the best products, I needed to get my act together. I needed to learn this camera. So I did the most reasonable thing I could think of. I drove across town, bought *Digital Photography for Dummies*, and sat down to read it over coffee. It was full of these terms that had defied my brain in that college class: F-stops. White balance. Focal length. Exposure modes. Shutter speeds. ISO. I read and read and read, and I reread when I didn't understand. And by the end of the day, the tool that had once frightened me to death was demystified.

I experimented with my new toy, shooting objects and textures around the house. I took it out to dinner and shot reflections off my water glass or silverware—abstract art kind of stuff. I shot portraits of Shannon, who was still my best, though not-so-willing model. She hated (and still hates) having her photo taken, but, thankfully, she let me. I'd take the same photo of her a dozen ways, and she'd smile through it all. She'd flip through the photos with me, too, and she'd give me honest feedback. She was the best model, the kind blessed with both beauty and brains.

Just about the time I figured out how to use my camera (at least sort of), Universal Records South called. Steven Delopoulos of the band Burlap to Cashmere needed a new website, album packaging, tour merchandise—the works. And for it he wanted a professional, multilocation photo shoot in New York City. They wondered whether I'd be interested in the gig, and I jumped on it despite the fact I still wasn't quite sure how to ensure proper exposure. (I hadn't yet learned to use the camera's internal light meter. I must have skipped that part of *Digital Photography for Dummies*.)

It was my first professional photography gig, and I didn't want to screw it up too badly, so I hired my friend Darci McCoy—an actual photographer—as my photography assistant. She brought her film camera to the photo shoot—a very high-end, professional, medium-format camera—and with our two cameras we shot Steven all day in New York. As excited as I was to work with Steven, it turned out that I was more in awe of Darci and her medium-format camera. Her mechanical know-how was amazing.

We made our way home after the shoot, processed the photos, and delivered them to Universal. They flipped out when they saw the photos, and so did I. They were absolutely gorgeous. Timeless.

So this is what it means to be a real photographer with a ridiculously rad camera.

That was a turning point. Months later, I decided to invest in an 8.0-megapixel Canon DSLR. Then came more testing, more shots of textures, more portraits of Shannon. I carried that camera with me everywhere I went, and with every click of the shutter button, I became more convinced I was making my way toward a new career. By 2005, photography was all I wanted to do.

In hindsight, I see how my life was beginning to resemble a collection of Photoshop layers—one idea laid over a previous idea laid over the one before. Underneath my newfound love for photography was that photo shoot in the park with Darci. But I wouldn't have booked that photo shoot without Pixelgrazer. I wouldn't have started Pixelgrazer without Shannon and Jimmy Abegg. I wouldn't have introduced myself to Jimmy Abegg without my love of art. I wouldn't have known of Jimmy if my father hadn't brought home those copies of *CCM Magazine*.

One thing led to another led to another, layer by layer by layer. And while each layer was important, one was imperative—my abstract-art-loving Yoda, Jimmy. He was the unexpected mentor I never knew I needed, the one who told me that I had what it took, that I should follow my ideas and see where they took me. That advice was priceless, and his belief in me helped me overcome my questions and take the leap of faith into forming my own freelance design company. But he didn't just stop there. He encouraged me to learn my craft, to pick up tools that could keep me on the cutting edge, and to become technically proficient. And as I followed his lead, I discovered new possibilities.

Finding someone who's a little farther down the road, someone who has walked a similar path and who will pour his experience into you, is a kind of grace. A priceless gift. Such selfless mentors nudge us in the right direction, add layers to our lives. And so often they give us the courage we need to explore the unknown. Because of Jimmy's influence, I'm not afraid to try new things, follow crazy ideas, or learn a new skill. I'm unafraid to add new layers to my life.

But there's a catch to this truth. Unless we choose to accept that we need a mentor, that we have something to learn in the first place, those mentors, those lessons and layers, will find someone else. Without the humility it takes to listen to and follow the sages in our lives, we won't grow into the work God has for us.

I'll always be grateful for the gift of grace Jimmy has been to me over the years. And following his lead, I try to encourage other young creatives to take the next step, to jump into their fears and embrace new possibilities.

So who's your mentor, the person who pushes you to take calculated risks and chase new ideas? Who is adding layers of depth to your life? If you don't have someone like Jimmy, you might be robbing yourself of a necessary layer, a layer that might create a more complete portrait of possibilities. And if you're the one a little farther down the road and you aren't giving back, you might be robbing someone else.

SELFLESS MENTORS NUDGE US IN THE RIGHT DIRECTION, ADD LAYERS TO OUR LIVES. AND SO OFTEN THEY GIVE US THE COURAGE WE NEED TO EXPLORE THE UNKNOWN.

Chapter 5

JUMPING OUT OF A MOVING VEHICLE

Creativity is just connecting things. When you ask
creative people how they did something, they feel a
little guilty because they didn't really do it, they just saw
something. It seemed obvious to them after a while.
—STEVE JOBS

A couple of years into my career as a graphic designer, everything
was running as if on autopilot—even me. Wake up. Call the clients.
Design a website. Collect the money. Wash. Rinse. Repeat.

Pinnix and I had created a well-oiled machine in Pixelgrazer,
and I was proud of that machine. We'd started with nothing but

our own ideas, the raw materials of our internal world, and we'd taken those raw materials and built something viable, a company with a reputation for creativity and artistry. We were in demand, and our websites were some of the most talked about in the local industry. And though perhaps I should have celebrated the success, should have capitalized on it and begun thinking through ways to scale up and expand, I didn't.

Maybe my vision was too small. Maybe other ideas were hijacking my focus. Maybe I'd exhausted my interest in web design. Maybe I was bored. Maybe—most likely—all those things were true.

I'd spent years learning the tips and tricks of graphic design, and I'd had fun doing it. But as I sat behind a desk day after day, using those same old tricks to create album covers, websites, merch, whatever, I found myself wanting a new challenge. I wanted to step out of the sandbox and onto the beach.

I carried my camera with me everywhere I went in those days, and when I wasn't shooting portraits of clients, I was shooting whatever was in front of me. I shot landscapes, buildings, folks on the street going about their everyday lives. I found the courage to ask my friends and family if I could nab portraits of them too. Everything was fair game. And when I imported the images into Photoshop, I was able to manipulate them in ways I never would have imagined in my college photography class. I could adjust the exposure, the tint, the color saturation. I could use the dodge and the burn tools to regulate exposure with more precision than I ever could in the darkroom—not that I'd been all that skilled at it in the darkroom. I could play with the lighting curves, increase the highlights, decrease the shadows.

As my comfort behind the camera grew, more and more

Pixelgrazer clients asked whether I was open to bookings, and they didn't just want portraits for album covers or merch, either. They needed promotional photos and headshots, portraits meant to capture them in their best light. I agreed to do those shoots even though they weren't necessarily part of Pixelgrazer's core business. And when I came into the office and noticed a photography day on a calendar—a day to leave the office and get out into the world—I could barely contain my excitement.

As I grew my photography portfolio, I booked more and more jobs. Some of those jobs took me on the road and brought me to new cities, where I met new people. I found myself outside for hours on end. I learned to tackle complex compositions and lighting issues on the fly. I learned how to fix exposure issues in postproduction. Photography was scratching an itch I hadn't known I had.

Finally one day, and after a shoot in downtown Nashville, I returned to the office and gave the news to Pinnix. I didn't want to design websites anymore. I was tired of designing album covers. It was time to turn the reins over to him and dedicate myself to photography full-time.

Pinnix listened, nodded, asked whether I was sure. I said yes, and he nodded again. "We'll have to figure out a transition plan," he said, without a hint of angst or animosity. He didn't wring his hands. He didn't throw a guilt trip on me, didn't say, "*You* invited *me* into this" or "How do you expect me to finish all the work in process?" Instead, he set to sorting out his strategy for moving Pixelgrazer forward without me.

My last day as a graphic designer was March 31, 2005. I can't recall the last website I built, the last pixel I grazed for the company I'd started. I can't remember the last client call I took. I don't remember any heaviness as I turned the keys to the kingdom over to Jeremy Pinnix, my partner for those few incredible years. Instead, I recall walking out the door, a world of possibility in front of me. I also remember the feeling in my stomach as the realization hit me: I'd just left a successful company, my metaphorical baby that would one day provide for my actual babies. I'd given it up to pursue some new dream, and who knew whether that would work out?

This brings me to a sort of confession. Risk takers, creatives, entrepreneurs—we usually act as if we have supreme confidence in our ideas, our art. We share our more notable successes as if we knew the ideas were solid gold from the beginning. But here's what risk takers too often gloss over, forget, or simply refuse to admit: when you leave the comfort of the known to pursue a yet unrealized dream, the questions, doubts, and fears break like waves over you.

That's exactly what happened to me hours into my new full-time photography career. I couldn't help wondering what I had done.

Have I made an enormous mistake?

Is this worth the risk?

If the phone doesn't ring, if I can't land enough jobs, what will this do to me financially, mentally, emotionally?

True to form, though, Shannon never questioned. She said we'd be all right, said this was the time to take the leap. She had a stable career as a physical therapist, we didn't have kids yet, and if it didn't work out, we could always find other jobs, other opportunities. Besides, this *would* work, she said. I had too much passion for it to fail. And whether it was true or not, I believed her.

I called my dad to tell him I'd officially walked away from Pixelgrazer and started my new gig as a full-time freelance photographer. He might have been concerned. He might have wondered whether I'd be as stable, as secure. If he did, he didn't share his reservations. Instead, he congratulated me. All things were possible, he said.

I put out the word that I was a full-time photographer, and I was over the moon when friends and former clients started reaching out and asking if I was taking bookings. My calendar filled, and before long I had shoots scheduled in New York and Los Angeles. Bigger labels called, asking whether I'd be open to shooting their artists. And it wasn't just musicians and record labels calling. A month into my photography career, my friend Barrett Ward called. He was the founder of the Mocha Club, a nonprofit fighting extreme poverty in Africa, and he wondered whether I'd be interested in traveling overseas to shoot their work. I agreed, and within days I received another call, this time from Blood:Water, a humanitarian organization providing African communities with access to clean water and health care. They'd heard I was traveling across the pond and asked whether I would extend my African trip. Would I be interested in shooting Blood:Water's work?

Would I ever.

My photography business's organic, word-of-mouth marketing campaign was unplanned and unexpected. It was coming together faster than I could have imagined, and I had no idea how to manage it all. I didn't have a clear business plan and hadn't thought through all the particulars. To complicate matters, I was terrible with accounting and small-business finance. So even though I had a clear artistic vision, I still doubted. No matter how much confidence I projected, I carried a lot of anxiety just below the surface. What if I wasn't good enough to pull it all off?

I was fighting for air in the fear and doubt of my newest business venture when I stepped off the plane from my trip to Africa with Mocha Club. I drove home, excited to see Shannon. She was excited to see me too. She had some news. Some of the biggest news of my life, actually. She was pregnant with our first son, Adler.

My heart exploded in joy, but then the fear came, the suffocating stress. But I made a conscious choice to not let my own skepticism get in the way. I owed it to myself, to Shannon, and to our coming child to push through the fear and anxiety and into my creative vision and skill. I owed it to us to do it wisely, too, and knowing I didn't have the business skills to organize it all, I made the smartest decision of my career. I called Michael Moore. (No, not the filmmaker. The *other* Michael Moore, who would become my own personal business ninja.)

Weeks into my new business, I'd asked my friend Matt Huesmann whether he knew a good accountant, and he gave me Michael's name. As it turned out, Michael wasn't an accountant; he was a jack-of-all-trades business guru, and after a few conversations, he agreed to take me as a client. If I'd known what I was getting in Michael—a numbers guy, strategist, accountant, business manager, investor, silent partner, and friend—I might not have been so nervous. If I'd known I was hiring someone who believed in me more than I believed in myself, I wouldn't have carried so much doubt in the early days of my business.

I've always been a bit of a self-starter, the kind of person who can't help but follow his own ideas, even if there's no solid plan and no guarantee those ideas will pan out. And if I do create a solid project or a good business vehicle, that doesn't mean I'll ride that vehicle to the end. Sometimes I'll jump from it, even when it's still humming along, even if I don't know what's waiting for me after the fall, and even if there's anxiety and trepidation in the jumping.

I've learned to trust my creative instincts over the years. I've always been willing to learn new skills, use new tools, hire or partner with others to compensate for my weaknesses, and explore new career opportunities. Even when the safe thing meant sticking with what I knew, even if it meant less anxiety, stress, or uncertainty, I would still take a calculated risk if that risk meant following a more compelling, more interesting, or more meaningful idea or opportunity.

Now in my forties, I've been approached by a number of folks who have grown weary of their careers. Musicians have told me they're tired of the grind, the travel, the constant demand for new content. Lawyers have said they can't keep churning out the hours, can't keep spitting out mundane briefs. Graphic designers and photographers have told me they're bored behind the computer screen or camera.

And how do I respond? I've told the musicians to put down the guitar and go back to school or move into a different area in the industry. I've counseled the lawyers to hang up their suits—to work for themselves or start a consulting company or something. I've encouraged the graphic designers and photographers to jump into a new industry altogether. Retool, I've told them all. Start something exciting and new. And without fail, time and time again they tell me, "I couldn't possibly. This is all I know."

Pardon me while I respectfully disagree.

There are a million reasons to avoid starting something new, a million reasons why sticking with what you know is more practical or more responsible or more *whatever*. There are a million reasons to limit your possibilities. But so often, those limitations are born in fear—fear of the unknown, fear of instability, fear of failure. Fear of the questions that haunt you just like they did me.

But what if?

What if you *could* start over? What if you could leave the angst of your personal rat race and do something more fulfilling? What if you knew you wouldn't starve? What if you believed you were possible? What if you could surround yourself with others who would help you believe you were possible or who could bring skills to the table you might not have? Then what decision would you make?

Don't get me wrong. There are some very good and practical reasons not to jump out of a moving vehicle. (Would I have jumped if I'd had four kids back then? Maybe not. Or maybe I would have at least taken a little more time unbuckling my seat belt.) But while you're riding in that vehicle, there's still no reason *not* to learn a new skill, and there is no reason to avoid implementing that skill in new and meaningful ways. Who knows? As you gain mastery of that skill, maybe you'll see new opportunities open up. That's how it worked for me with photography. In fact, that's how it's worked throughout my career.

In the days after leaving Pixelgrazer, I continued to fill my calendar with shoots, knowing I'd made the right move, even if I was starting all over in a completely new field. I made that trip to Africa. The photos were even better than I'd expected. And somewhere along the way, those photos came across the desk of Cameron Strang, the founder of *Relevant* magazine. Cameron reached out and asked if they could turn the project into a book entitled *Hope in the Dark*. I'd only been a full-time photographer for a month, had made an overseas trip with a camera I barely knew how to use, and somehow I'd just landed my first book deal.

I believe that was a little message from God, a way to show me I was on the right path. I could push through the fear. I'd be all right. So I kept following that path, and work kept coming—work I would have missed had I let fear get in the way and stayed with the safe thing. And though I didn't know it at the time, that single move—the move from graphic design to photography—would prove to be the single most important career decision I would ever make. It was the next step in my unconventional entrepreneurial path, one that would turn me into the last thing I would have ever expected—a purpose hotelier.

THERE ARE A
MILLION REASONS
TO LIMIT YOUR
POSSIBILITIES.
BUT SO OFTEN,
THOSE LIMITATIONS
ARE BORN IN FEAR—
FEAR OF THE
UNKNOWN, FEAR
OF INSTABILITY,
FEAR OF FAILURE.

Chapter 6

FAKE IT TILL YOU MAKE IT

All you need in this life is ignorance and
confidence; then success is sure.

—ATTRIBUTED TO MARK TWAIN

I was driving down the interstate when my phone vibrated. It was a
cold call from an unknown number, but I answered it anyway. Isn't
every cold call an opportunity waiting to happen?

"This is Caryn Weiss from Weiss Artists. Is this Jeremy Cowart?"
the caller asked. She explained she was a photography agent in Los
Angeles, and she had stumbled across my work. "Truth be told," she
said, "you beat out several of my clients for the Rebecca St. James
shoot." She explained that she represented at least two other
photographers—professionals with amazing portfolios—who'd bid

for the same job I had. When she received the call that I'd won the gig, she had visited my website and started reviewing my portfolio.

"It's really impressive," she said. "I love your work. Do you have an agent?"

Wait—so a photography agent is a real thing?

Without missing a beat she said, "Go look at my website—I think you'll like it—and then get back to me. I'd love to represent you."

Back in the office I reviewed Caryn's website, and she was right. I liked it. A lot. In fact, I was blown away at the talent she represented and the images they'd captured. She represented photographers who shot television and movie sets, photographed A-list celebrities and supermodels. Those photographers were true artists who captured perfect images. And she wanted to represent me, whose photographic background included a D grade, an armoire shoot, and a *For Dummies* book.

I didn't have the skills those other photographers had. I didn't have the tools.

Shouldn't I out my limitations? Shouldn't I give it to her straight? Nah.

I called her, told her I was in. She asked when I could get started, and I told her I was about to leave for Rwanda to partner on a project with Blood:Water. Could I start in two weeks? She agreed, said she'd hunt down some jobs for me. And just like that, I had an agent.

Weeks later, in an internet café in Butare, Rwanda, I received an e-mail from Caryn. I read it twice, then a third time. Was it real?

"I pitched you to Fox. You know how to light big sets, right?"

I knew next to nothing about lighting. I knew even less about shooting a large set.

Shouldn't I out my limitations? Shouldn't I give it to her straight?
Maybe. Maybe not.

"No problem," I wrote back. "When do we start?"

During the next few days in Butare, I shot for Blood:Water, and in the evenings I made my way back to that internet café to see whether Caryn had responded. A day passed. Another. And just when I thought I might have lost whatever job she'd pitched, I received another e-mail from her.

"Good news! You've been hired to shoot the set of the second season of *Prison Break*. You'll need to be on set in a week."

Electricity ran up my spine; I rubbed my arms and felt the goose bumps. My heart raced, the adrenaline doing its thing. A thousand thoughts came, then a thousand second thoughts.

I need to call Shannon.

I need to book tickets from Rwanda to the set.

Should I watch the first season of Prison Break *so I have an idea of what I'm walking into?*

What am *I walking into?*

How will I pull this off?

I connected my iPhone to the café Wi-Fi and began downloading the first season of *Prison Break*. As I waited out the eternity it took for each episode to download, I considered my life.

Haven't things always worked out, even when I didn't know how they would?

Can't I figure out how to manage a little lighting?

I brushed the questions aside as I watched the download status crawl to the finish line. After what seemed like a decade of downloading episodes at almost dial-up speeds, I made my way back to the Blood:Water team, ready to share the news.

After dinner and a long night of conversation, I climbed into the bed in my mud hut. Outside I heard the sounds of the people—the singing, the laughing, the pounding of drums. I was thousands of miles from home, an ocean away from the American entertainment industry, but thanks to modern technology, I was ready to start researching. I pulled the mosquito net around me, put my headphones in, and pressed play on my phone. Within minutes I was sucked into the world of Lincoln and Michael and Veronica and Fernando.

Whether it was the television show or the excitement, I'll never know, but I don't think I slept a wink that night. And every night after that in Rwanda was the same. After a long day of water wells and clinics and smiling children, I'd crawl into bed, pull the net around me, and watch American television, sucked into insomnia by the excitement of it all.

Will Dr. Tancredi find out that Michael doesn't actually have diabetes?

Is Aldo really Lincoln's father?

Are the guards going to walk into the break room right when the Fox River Eight are in the middle of digging the hole?

I quickly realized I wasn't scheduled to shoot any old show. I was scheduled to shoot a great show! And as I continued to watch episode after episode, I became a fan.

A few days passed, and I boarded a plane back to the States. Heading home after any overseas trip to a developing country will give you culture shock, so imagine the culture shock of flying directly to Dallas and arriving at the hotel where the cast of *Prison Break* was hanging out in the lobby. What's more, I had finished the last episode minutes before touching down in Dallas, so seeing my new favorite television characters sitting in the lobby was quite a trip. I glanced from person to person, remembering each of their character arcs.

You just overdosed.

And you just got left behind.

And you just got your hand chopped off.

My overactive imagination struggled to separate fiction from reality—that is, until I walked over and introduced myself to Lincoln and Michael and Veronica and Fernando (or Dominic and Wentworth and Robin and Amaury). I told them I was their new photographer, and each was so gracious. I followed them to the elevator, and as we stepped in, we proceeded to have totally normal conversation about the World Cup and the movie *Wedding Crashers.*

I couldn't sleep that night. Maybe it was jet lag. Maybe it was because I couldn't believe my luck. Maybe it was because I had no idea how to light a television set—but hey, how hard could it be? I shook off my worry, tried my best to catch a few winks, and made my way to the set early the next morning.

I was about to take on the world of television photography. I was about to make a name for myself. I was about to blow the world away. I was sure of all these things until I was escorted onto the soundstage, at which point I realized I was screwed.

A sea of gear stretched out at least a hundred feet in front of me. Lights. C-stands. Sandbags. Grips. Booms. Strobes. Power packs. Things with wheels. Things that looked like dividers. Things that were made of plastic and metal and space-age polymers that were made for . . . what?

I scanned the rest of the enormous soundstage and saw that it had been divided into no fewer than half a dozen sets. Michael's apartment. The lobby of City Hall. The police station. Frank's bedroom. Was that the interior of a train?

"Follow me. I'll take you to the second soundstage," one of the four assistants assigned to me said. "There are a couple more sets over in that one."

More sets?

More lights?

More things I've never seen?

When I accepted the job, I knew I would be shooting all the publicity photos that *Prison Break* would use to market the show, and I'd hoped to be able to shoot while they were filming the scenes. I'd heard that photographers who shot the action stills for a show tended to shoot this way and that, in those cases, camera silencers were used so the photographer's clicks didn't interfere with sound recording. That way the photographer could use the same lighting the director and cinematographer used for each scene, to ensure there was uniformity. But I wasn't shooting during filming, so I didn't have access to the cinematographic lighting. I hadn't realized that when I took the job, but it now became clear as the assistant showed me around the set.

She showed me where the actors were going to pose and reenact scenes for me to shoot and told me the sea of lighting equipment was all for me. I had access to whatever I wanted, and we'd light each set to my taste, from scratch. She smiled as if she were giving me some huge creative gift, and today, after years of shooting photography around the world, I know why. Having the equipment, budget, and freedom to set my own lighting schemes is an artistic dream come true. But back then, since I was little more than a novice who had lit only a few interior spaces with professional equipment, it was anything but a dream. In fact, it was a nightmare.

"You have a whole day to pre-light, and the actors will be here tomorrow morning," the assistant said, but all I heard was, "You're in way over your head, Cowart."

I took a deep breath and wiped a bead of sweat off my forehead. Then I mustered up my courage, looked at the crew, and said, "Let's get to work."

After watching the first season of the show, I knew the general feel of the cinematography—the use of shadows, the subtle illumination with different hues, the use of high angles for shooting so the less authoritative characters looked smaller. I walked from set to set, thinking through which characters would be where and how best to capture their personas. I closed my eyes and could visualize the shots in my head, even though I didn't know how to create them with all that equipment. But my crew didn't know that, so I faked it the best I could.

"We'll definitely shoot Lincoln in here, so we need low-key lighting. Make it moody and dark," I said. I watched one of the guys start sorting through light stands and clamps and who knows what else.

"Sara will be in here, and I'll want her softened considerably," I said. "It should feel warm." I listened as two other assistants talked through whether to use barn doors with diffusion paper or umbrellas or silks. One asked my opinion. I nodded and said, "Whatever you think," and off they went. I laughed as I realized my professionally trained lighting assistants were teaching me the tricks of the trade.

I made my way through both soundstages and told the crew

my rough ideas for each of the actors. I watched as they sorted, mounted, adjusted, and tested all the equipment. I watched closely as they worked, and I'm sure they thought I was examining their work to ensure everything was up to my standards. In reality, though, I was noting their lighting choices, placement, configurations, and technique. I was watching how they put things together and which gear went with what. I was listening to them talk about their reasoning as they climbed up and down the lighting truss. I took mental notes. They were teaching me lighting. They just didn't know it.

As promised, the actors showed up the next day. And thanks to my crew (who should have received enormous raises and honorary doctoral degrees for teaching me everything I know about lighting), I was ready. Through thousands of shots, my visions came to life. Somehow I pulled off the shoot and came out on the other side of it unscathed.

The job ended, and I said good-bye to the cast and crew and boarded a plane back to Nashville. During the short flight home, I considered the lessons I'd learned on the soundstage. I'd taken a job that was beyond my skill set, and I'd made it through without anyone knowing I was clueless. And by the end of it all, I'd actually learned the tricks of the trade. I could now light a soundstage with the best of them.

I wondered what would have happened if I had told Caryn I didn't know how to light big sets. How would it have turned out if I'd faked an illness on the first day of shooting and sat in my hotel room, studying lighting equipment and techniques on the internet? What if I'd told the production team I wasn't their guy? I wasn't sure, but I was glad I hadn't done that.

Why didn't I? Because my belief in my capacity was bigger than my fear.

As I considered the lessons of that shoot, my mind wandered into Jeremyland. It had been a scary moment, a moment when I stood on the edge of a cliff and had to muster up the courage to take the leap of faith. But then, I'd taken my fair share of faith leaps in my younger days in Hendersonville—from those high cliffs over the lake.

I remembered those days so clearly. The nervous jitters. The push from the edge. The floating in my stomach. The epic splash into the water. The climb back up the cliff to do it all over again. And as I had scaled higher and higher cliffs, as I'd jumped and jumped and jumped, I had gained access to the confidence that lives right underneath the fear. And my *Prison Break* shoot had let me access that same confidence again.

When I returned to Nashville, I processed the shots from *Prison Break* and sent them to the client. They were elated. Over the moon. Caryn called, and we talked about those photos. She was floored by them, and she said she'd start passing my name around to other television studios. It was a real sweet spot, and she was excited to have another photographer in her agency who was able to shoot big sets.

We never talked about the fact that I hadn't known how to light a set before that job. I'd taken the whole "fake it till you make it" mantra to the extreme, and in the process I'd discovered I could catch anything the photography world could throw at me.

Was that the actual truth? I didn't really know, but right then and there I made up my mind. I'd never say no to a project or idea simply because I thought I couldn't do it. I would dare to take on more complicated projects and bigger ideas because talent without audacity is a waste.

All of us have *Prison Break* moments in life, moments when we can either walk away from the cliff's edge or take an audacious risk. When those moments come, we can find ourselves paralyzed with fear, crippled by self-doubt, or overly concerned with the prospect of failure. But if I've learned anything over the years, it's that when we exercise our audacity, worlds of possibility open up.

The possibility of failure? Sure. But the possibility of wild success? Absolutely. In those successes, we'll discover new opportunities to say yes. And as we follow those yeses, those opportunities (and the opportunities that flow from those opportunities), we'll find ourselves wrestling with bigger ideas, grander dreams, and greater purpose.

How do I know? It's the truth that's shaped my life.

When was the last time you pushed aside the fear, the self-doubt, the prospect of failure, and exercised your audacious yes?

When was the last time you took a risk that required you to sink or swim?

If it's been too long, look for those opportunities in the world around you. Look for ways to use your talents in bigger ways, to agree to things that might seem out of your reach. Say yes to something grand and see what happens. Don't you owe it to yourself?

TALENT WITHOUT AUDACITY IS A WASTE.

Chapter 7

STAIRWAY TO NOWHERE

First, think. Second, dream. Third, believe. And finally, dare.

–FOUR PRINCIPLES OF WALT DISNEY

If you'd have been an invisible person in the room when Sony called about shooting publicity photos for Chris Botti, you'd have thought I'd won the lottery. In some sense, it felt as if I had. Botti, a jazz trumpeter who had toured with music legends such as Paul Simon and Sting, had been one of my favorite musical artists for years, and I was being asked to photograph his three-day live concert DVD taping in Los Angeles. As if that weren't cool enough, there would be a full orchestra, and a slew of famous artists were slated to perform with him, including Paula Cole, Gladys Knight, and Sting himself. I was not even a year into my career as a full-time photographer, and doors were opening I'd never imagined possible. It was all so much more than I could have asked or imagined.

As the live photographer at a concert, I'd be out in the audience with a long lens. I packed my gear accordingly, but I also brought along some lighting strobes and my best portrait lens in case an opportunity presented itself. I kissed my wife good-bye and flew to the Golden State with Botti and Sting's studio albums downloaded onto my iPod.

When I arrived at the Wilshire Theatre on the morning of the first day of taping, a runner showed me around backstage—catering, security offices, dressing rooms, merchandise storage, loading dock, reserved area for meet and greets. I was then introduced to the art director, who handed me the set list and corresponding light cues and then told me about her vision for the shoot—create black-and-white options in postproduction, capitalize on the effects of the haze machine, get a good mix of silhouette shots, and don't ignore the orchestra.

After we ran through it all, she said, "One more thing. Don't shoot portraits of the artists backstage. You're the live photographer; you should only be shooting live concert shots from good vantage points in the audience." She handed me a card on a lanyard. "Here's your all-access pass."

But I want to take portraits. I even brought my stuff.

That's what I wanted to say. But before I could get the words out, she was gone.

I brushed aside the disappointment and decided to look for opportunity, for possibility. As I did, I noticed the organized chaos of being backstage at a concert. There were so many moving pieces, especially at an event like this that would span multiple days and involve such a magnitude of star power. As the day went on, the number of people running around like headless chickens backstage had increased to the point where no one was paying attention to anyone else. And in that chaotic atmosphere, a question took hold: *Can I sneak in those portraits I want, even if I have to break a rule or two?*

While Botti and the orchestra took the stage for mic checks and blocking, I walked the theater to get a feel for different angles, the lighting, the focal lengths I'd need. I made my way through the auditorium and the balcony as if in a dream, noting the gold fixtures, the dark wood paneling, the ornate chandeliers, and the red velvet curtain lining the expansive stage. There were only twelve hundred seats—a relatively small concert venue for stars like Sting and Knight—but the effect was regal all the same.

I took a few test shots, and as I did, I noticed Sting walking onstage. I stayed on him until he finished his mic check, and then it was like a revolving door of talent as Paula Cole, Gladys Knight, Burt Bacharach, David Foster, Renee Olstead, and Jill Scott came onto the stage to practice their songs with Chris. I couldn't believe I was among so many legends, and it was all I could do to keep the camera steady as I shot.

I'm never going to be in a room with all of these amazing artists ever again.

I have to get them to pose for me.

Imagine having a portrait of Sting in my portfolio.

The art director said I couldn't.

But maybe just one.

What's the worst that could happen?

I wandered around backstage, trying to find a spot where I

could set up a mini portrait studio. It needed to be inconspicuous, in a place that didn't have a lot of foot traffic (as in, somewhere the art director wouldn't go), and that's when I spotted a stairwell. I walked down the steps and found nothing but a wall at the bottom. It was a tiny stairwell to nowhere.

Perfect.

Am I allowed to use this?

Wasn't I given an all-access pass?

I sneaked a few lights down the stairs; they illuminated the white cinder blocks and exposed electrical conduit. It wasn't the ideal backdrop, but it was certainly better than nothing. Then I formulated a plan. Over the course of the next three days, when I wasn't shooting concert photos, I'd "casually" walk around backstage, hoping to strike up conversations with potential portrait subjects and perhaps talk them into posing for me.

Would it work? I didn't know, but I had to try.

On the second day of the concert, Sting stepped backstage after singing "My Funny Valentine," and I knew it was the opportunity I'd been waiting for. I took a deep breath, pushed back the memory of the art director's *no*, and made my way over to him.

"Hi. I'm here shooting for Sony," I said (which was true, thank you very much). "I'd love to take a quick portrait of you."

He smiled—even with a smile, he had that classic Sting smolder—and he said two magic words: "Okay, sure."

He followed me down into my not-so-professional portrait studio. I walked the steps, legs loose from so much adrenaline, and I clenched my fists in hopes my hands would stop shaking. Starstruck as I was, I might have asked him some ridiculous questions. I pulled myself together, though, and managed not to say anything ridiculously memorable. When he was in position, I took just ten photos. I thanked him and walked him back up the stairwell, where Tom Cruise and Katie Holmes happened to be standing. (What was my life? And why couldn't I manage the courage to ask them for a couple of shots?)

The concert ended, I turned my portfolio of shots over to the art director, and I made my way back to Nashville. A few days passed, and she called. She told me she'd seen the photos of Sting and all the other artists I'd snuck portraits of.

Oh no, I thought. *Here we go.*

They were amazing, she said, thanking me over and over again. They were the highlight of the portfolio, some of the best shots of the show. And then she outed her own secret: "To be honest, I told you not to shoot the artists because I didn't have the courage to ask them if it would be okay."

It was an empowering admission, and I took it as a sign that I should trust my instincts even if those instincts cut against the creative direction. What's more, the experience gave me the confidence and the portfolio to make another big ask just a couple of months later.

I'd heard the CMT Music Awards were being hosted in Nashville, just as they were every year. And though this shouldn't have surprised a Tennessee-born-and-bred boy like me, especially one whose career involved shooting country musicians on occasion, the award ceremony hadn't been on my radar. Truth is, I liked the personalities of those country musicians more than I liked their music, which might be more of a commentary on my lack of taste than it is on their music. All that to say, I'd never paid much attention to the awards show—that is, until I had the idea to set up a portrait booth at the show just as I had at the Botti concert.

I cold-called CMT.

"Hi, I'm a photographer in town, Jeremy Cowart. Y'all are doing the upcoming CMT Awards show, and I'd like to set up a photo booth and take portraits of all the artists coming through. Can I come do that for you?"

They were gracious and asked to see my portfolio. I sent it over, Sting portrait and all, and then they called me back and told me yes. (I assume Sting won them over.) Who knew it'd be that easy? I didn't. It just goes to show that you never know until you ask.

The night of the awards ceremony came around, and I lugged my gear to the venue early to allow plenty of time to set up my booth. I hung a gray seamless backdrop—much classier than the cinder blocks and conduit at the Wilshire Theatre—and placed a stool right in front of it for the artists to sit on. I had my tripod and softbox (a lighting device) and was ready to roll when people started to arrive.

From that moment on, it was an endless parade of who's who in the world of country music. Brooks & Dunn, Sugarland, Alan Jackson, Brad Paisley, Hank Williams, Blake Shelton, and the new *American Idol* winner Carrie Underwood. As each of them walked by, I politely asked if I could shoot their portraits and, God bless 'em, every one of them agreed. I kept the sessions to two or three minutes because I didn't want to be a bother. Besides, getting them in and out allowed me opportunities to shoot more artists, even the up-and-comers. The brevity paid off.

A new artist—some kid named Taylor Swift—walked past my booth. I didn't know who she was (she hadn't achieved world domination yet), but she looked as awestruck about being there as I did. That doe-in-the-headlights look was so endearing, and I asked her if she would sit for me. She agreed, probably thinking she couldn't say no, and I took a handful of photos, spending a total of two minutes with her. I thanked her. She thanked me. And then she disappeared into the sea of people backstage.

At the end of the shoot, I reviewed my photos. I loved them all, but of all the photos I took that night—heck, out of all the photos I took that year—hers was my favorite. In fact, it's the one people make the biggest fuss over to this day. And if I hadn't pushed through the fear of following my instincts at the Botti concert, if I hadn't worked through the nerves of asking Sting for an impromptu portrait, I wouldn't have had the portfolio to open the door to the CMT Music Awards show. And I never would have gotten that shot of Taylor Swift.

Early in my career, a photo industry professional told me about a photographer who'd bid to shoot Keith Urban. The photographer sent Urban his portfolio, and as the country music star leafed through the book, he ran across a photograph of Faith Hill. It was a terrible photo—too dim and a touch out of focus—but it didn't matter because it was still a photo of country superstar Faith Hill. According to the man who had firsthand account of the story, Urban hired the photographer on the spot. He wanted to work with the photographer who had worked with Faith Hill. And who could blame him?

"Sometimes it doesn't matter how good you are," the industry vet said, "but who's in your portfolio."

That story stuck with me, probably because I didn't want to believe it. I wanted to believe my future success would come down to the quality and artistry of my work or the originality of my concepts. I wanted to believe that everyone started on the same playing field, and that talent was what would put me ahead. But the more I worked in the industry, the more I realized how true that advice was. And I realized that if I wanted to build a good portfolio of great subjects, I'd need to get over my nerves and make the big asks. The crazy asks. The "they might say no" asks.

Because what if they said yes?

I'll be the first to admit that the photo I took of Sting isn't amazing. It's a basic portrait. The Taylor Swift portrait is much the same. But to this day, industry professionals use both as talking points when discussing my work. "Jeremy shot Sting and Taylor," they'll say when introducing me to someone. They never share the story behind either of those shoots, of course. They don't say that I intentionally broke the only rule I was given to shoot Sting. (To be clear, I'm not promoting breaking all the rules, just the rules that limit creativity without reason.) They don't tell that I shot Taylor before anyone knew her and that the shoot came from a cold call. (I'm also not suggesting making cold calls without the skills to back them up.) Still, those two photos have opened more doors than I can count, and all because I was willing to take a risk and create an opportunity.

At the end of a commencement speech that Steve Jobs gave at Stanford in 2005, he told the graduates, "Stay hungry. Stay foolish." It's a quote I love, one that motivates me. The innovator's innovator was acknowledging that people don't always act sensibly when it comes to something they're deeply passionate about, and it's those people—the ones willing to go outside of their comfort zones, throw caution to the wind, and break the right rules—who pull off the craziest ideas. The ones willing to make the crazy ask, take the crazy shot, and leverage the results are the ones who realize the power of their possibilities.

I don't suppose I'll be asked to speak at Stanford's graduation anytime soon, but you've shelled out a few bucks for this book, so allow me to share my own sort of commencement address with you:

> Write down your ideas. Follow your ideas. Push past the nerves, muster the guts, and put yourself out there. Don't be afraid to be told no, and don't let anything shut you down. After all, what's the worst that can happen? And when you reap the rewards of those ideas, leverage, leverage, leverage them. Turn one opportunity into another. Push back the fear as you step into that opportunity too. Make your Sting moment. Find your Taylor Swift. Stay stupid and bold. Watch what happens. And never underestimate the power of the ask.

THE ONES
WILLING TO
MAKE THE CRAZY
ASK, TAKE THE
CRAZY SHOT, AND
LEVERAGE THE
RESULTS ARE
THE ONES WHO
REALIZE THE
POWER OF THEIR
POSSIBILITIES.

Part 3

PORTRAIT OF AN ARTIST AS A HEALER

Chapter 8

HOW HELPING CHANGED EVERYTHING

Love your neighbor as yourself.

—JESUS

My best ideas come to me in the shower. That's a weird sentence to write, but admit it: All of our best ideas come in the bathroom, right?

One day in 2008, I was taking my morning shower, and my mind was wandering, making loose connections. I thought about a viral video making the rounds, a video made by three pastors asking folks to conspire against the commercialism of Christmas. Buy less, they said. Give more. Give something valuable, like time or something made by hand. Take the money you've saved and give it to those in need.

Arms against the wall, head down, I watched the shower water fall in streams from the top of my head, and I considered what I might give. My thoughts wandered to my friend Chase Jarvis. A photographer in Seattle, he'd pulled together a huge gathering of everyday folks who wanted to learn photography or improve their photographic skills. He'd invited models and lighting specialists and then opened the doors to people who wanted to learn to shoot like professionals. The novice photographers got to work together, learn from each other, and gain experience in a professional setting.

The water was washing away the other cares of my everyday life, allowing me to focus on these two seemingly unrelated ideas— rethinking Christmas, and Chase's photographer gathering. That's when a stream of consciousness took over.

What can I do for Christmas that doesn't involve buying gifts?

I can take pictures for people.

What if I take pictures of people—like Chase did, but not of models?

What if, instead of models, I take pictures of folks who are down-and-out?

What if I give them the portrait as a gift?

What could it mean for someone to be given the dignity of a decent portrait?

And wouldn't it be amazing to invite my local photographer friends to help?

That was it—the idea. Fully formed. Crystal clear.

I stepped out of the shower, grabbed a towel, and made my way to Shannon. She was in the kitchen, making breakfast for Adler, who was playing with a truck at the breakfast table, and Eisley, our second child, who was sitting in her high chair. I shouted ideas down the hall as I walked toward her, barely able to contain them.

"Anyone with a camera could come out," I said, "and we could shoot portraits for people in need, maybe some who have never had their picture professionally taken. We could shoot them and then give them a print as a gift, for free. Maybe I could get hair and makeup artists to come out, too, to make people feel really special, like a million bucks. How cool would it be to give a struggling single mom the option to get all glammed up and have her picture taken? Or give unemployed people something they could send in with a résumé? We could call it Help-Portrait. You know, instead of self-portrait." (This was before self-portraits were called "selfies.")

I spit the ideas out as they came into my head. When I finally stopped talking, I looked at Shannon, her face coming into focus as I pulled out of my cave of ideas. She was crying—which floored me. As beautiful and empathetic and sensitive as my wife is, she's not really a crier.

"Yes, yes, yes," she said. "You have to do that."

You heard the lady, Cowart. Get to work.

I rushed back to my office, a small room next to our bedroom, and e-mailed a few photographers, then posted about the idea on Facebook. Would anyone be interested in participating in Help-Portrait? Ten photographers responded, and among them was Kyle Chowning, an acquaintance whom I really didn't know, but who would soon become a collaborator and close friend. He was all in, he said. And so were the others.

Now to find a venue.

I put out the call, and one of the volunteer photographers said he had a connection at a school in downtown Nashville that might be willing to provide space. Within a week we had the location locked down.

Now, how will we find our subjects?

Another friend responded and said he knew someone at a local homeless shelter. He offered to reach out and see if they'd help spread the word among their community. They agreed.

But how will we provide the prints to the subjects?

Another friend said he had an extra printer he could bring.

Another had a sister who did makeup.

Still another would bring his wife, who had a flair for doing hair.

How is this coming together so quickly?

On the first Saturday morning of December, we showed up at the school gym with our gear—cameras, tripods, seamless backgrounds, C-stands, and lights, all of which I'd learned how to use by now—unsure if anyone would come. But over the course of the day, sixty or so folks trickled in to have their portraits taken, which was fifty-nine more than I'd expected. The volunteers worked together to take the best shots of those who came, and when we weren't shooting or doing makeup or adjusting lighting, we enjoyed conversations with those who'd come to have their portraits taken. After each shoot we printed the portraits and handed them to our new friends. They took the prints and studied them, and their reaction was the same each time: smiles, laughter, tears.

The conversations I shared with those who had fallen on hard times worked on me throughout the day. They reminded me that we're all one bad break away from disadvantage, one economic downturn away from difficulty. As these men and women shared their stories with me, they taught me a lesson—that even in the most difficult circumstances, there is still room for joy.

I got home that night and shared the stories with Shannon, who hadn't been able to make the event. I shared that I felt as if I'd used photography that day to restore some people's dignity. I told her about how the subjects' stories had changed my paradigm, too, how they made me aware of my own advantage. "My cup runneth over," I said.

The week after our first Help-Portrait shoot, I posted a video of the event on Facebook. The video didn't go viral; in fact, it received only modest attention. A handful of likes. Eight comments. All of those comments, though, conveyed the same message: "If you do this again, I want to be part of it."

Do it again? I hadn't thought of that.

Maybe I should do it again.

What if I do it every year?

What if I spread the word?

Could this be global?

How would I even begin to organize that?

I honestly had my doubts. I didn't know whether Help-Portrait could be anything other than a Nashville event. So I ran the idea of expanding our little experiment by Kyle first, and then by my business manager, Michael. Both agreed we should give it a go. We'd seen its empowering, dignifying effects in action, and we'd experienced our own life changes in the process. How could we not ride this idea as far as it would go?

So I pushed back the questions and doubts and, with the support of Shannon and my friends, jumped in. Within weeks we started planning for the following year.

This time I upped my game and made a video breaking Help-Portrait down into understandable parts. On the screen, I shared:

> It's a really simple idea. It involves all photographers: beginners, amateurs, strobists, hobbyists, weekenders, gearheads, Flickr pros, professionals, and even legends. Here's the deal: on December 12 we all grab our cameras, we find people in need, and we take their pictures. And when the prints are ready, we deliver them. That's it.

I outlined the vision, shared how we'd be helping people who had never dreamed of having their portrait made—kids without their own families, patients at the children's hospital, single moms, the elderly, the homeless, even our own neighbors. And there was only one rule: we wouldn't share the photos or keep them for our portfolios or post them online. This was about giving *to* our neighbors, not taking *from* them.

In September I posted the video as a guest contributor on Scott Kelby's widely read photography blog, and I couldn't have predicted the reaction. The idea spread like wildfire within our industry, and I checked my e-mail inbox every day in disbelief. Photographers, hair and makeup artists, organizers, caterers, lighting pros, community volunteers—so many began to rally around the idea. Three months later, in just its second year, Help-Portrait events were held in forty-two countries, at more than five hundred locations. More than thirty-five hundred photographers participated, and five thousand volunteers gave away forty-one thousand portraits. (Remember, social media was still new. Instagram wasn't a thing, hardly anyone was tweeting, Facebook was in its infancy, and the now wildly popular "Humans of New York" didn't even exist.) And as incredible as the numbers were, the stories were even better.

In Nashville a girl with extensive facial scarring came to be photographed, and she shared how she'd been raised by an abusive father who dumped acid on her face as a form of punishment. She'd had the scars for as far back as she could remember, she said. We shot her portrait and then, pixel by pixel, photoshopped all her scars away so she could see what she looked like without her father's abuse. We handed her the portrait, and as she looked at her new face, she wept. It was a holy moment, a moment she had entrusted to us. In solidarity, we wept along with her.

And it wasn't just her story that left its mark. Photo by photo, portrait by portrait, the stories rolled in, and as they did, our hearts softened. Our privilege, our blessing, our luck (whatever you want to call it) was exposed. And with that exposure came a great weight.

We pushed forward into the third year, hoping to expand the project even more. And as word of mouth spread, that's exactly what happened.

Year after year—2010, 2011, 2012—we engaged in our annual Help-Portrait event. And the more we shot, the less emphasis there seemed to be on "Help" and the more emphasis there was on the "Portrait." We were framing people with stories, stories that created moments of connection.

In 2010 an immigrant asked me to photograph her and her four children, then photoshop a picture of her husband into the family portrait. A Pakistani who'd been killed in war, he'd died before the family could get a proper family portrait made. I finished that portrait and handed it to her in tears. Her husband had given his life in service to his country, and why? I whispered a prayer for her family, but I whispered a prayer for peace on earth too.

Lord, teach me to be a means of peace.

A year later, a seven-year-old girl at an orphanage in Pematangsiantar, Indonesia, wrote after attending a Help-Portrait event. "Now I have a photograph for the first time, and I will show this to my mother when I meet her someday," she said. A girl without a family in a developing country, and she still carried hope. How was this kind of hope possible? Couldn't I learn something from her?

Lord, give me the hope of this little girl.

I could catalog the stories—the mother who received the first photo of her special-needs son smiling, the woman fresh out of rehab who wanted a photo to mark the next chapter of her life, my photographer buddy Sasha Leahovcenco, who traveled to Chukotka, Russia, to take portraits for a tribe of reindeer herders— but it would take countless pages.

And how could I possibly convey the holiness of each of those stories?

How could I summarize the breadth and depth of human joy, pain, and struggle we captured in those photos?

How could I ever convey how much those stories changed me?

I knew my Help-Portrait idea was powerful the minute it hit me mid-shower. I just didn't know how powerful. I knew images could convey stories and stir the emotions of an audience. But after ten years and nearly a million Help-Portrait photographs, I've come to see that photographs do more than tell a story. They have the power to restore dignity and expose privilege. They have the power to shift trajectories or paradigms or destinies—the destiny of the subject, the destiny of the photographer, the destiny of every person who views the photograph. Images change people.

Over the years I've considered that moment in the shower, how the idea came to me in the quietest, most private place—the place where social media, my phone, and the news of the day couldn't reach me. By allowing my mind to wander and following the loose connections, a seemingly impossible idea came together. And if I hadn't tuned out distractions and given myself that space to process, the idea might never have come together. I might never have heard the stories of those Help-Portrait models. I might not have allowed those stories to shift my worldview. I might never have started looking for ways to be a microphone for others, might not have found ways to share the stories of the human struggle.

Possibilities hide in all of us, but so often we don't carve out quiet places to let our minds wander into them. We fill our homes, our cars, our neighborhood walks, every quiet space with noise—music, video, social media, whatever. Because of that noise, that distraction, we end up missing the big ideas, the ones that might restore dignity or expose privilege or shift paradigms. We end up missing the ideas that could change us and make us better.

Do you allow yourself moments of quiet, space for your mind to wander? If you don't, consider giving it a try, even if only for a few minutes a day. See what connections you make, what ideas come from those connections. Map out one of those ideas, even if it seems crazy. Follow it and see what happens.

Listening in the quiet, listening to ideas—this might be the most important practice for any creator. It's the practice that might change your trajectory if you'll let it. It did mine.

PHOTOGRAPHS
DO MORE
THAN TELL
A STORY.....
IMAGES
CHANGE
PEOPLE.

Chapter 9

WHEN THE
WORLD SHAKES

I will not follow where the path may lead, but I will go
where there is no path, and I will leave a trail.

—MURIEL STRODE

In early 2010, Shannon and I were sitting on the couch, our two
toddlers toddling around the living room, and we were glued to
the CNN coverage about the catastrophic earthquake that had
just struck Haiti. As footage flashed across the screen of collapsed
houses and destroyed buildings and crumbled roads, it became
clear we were watching a disaster of epic proportions. We were
watching the decimation of an entire country.

We listened as correspondents spoke of the insufficient foun-
dations of the fallen Haitian structures, the rising death tolls and

overwhelmed morgues, the search and rescue efforts that appeared to be secondary to the government's efforts to stop all the violence and looting. And as we watched, we couldn't help but put ourselves in their shoes, so many of whom were parents. We couldn't help but cry and lift Haiti up in prayer.

As the hours trickled by, all the news outlets reported the same things. Hundreds of thousands of buildings damaged or destroyed. Tens of thousands of bodies recovered. Interviews with experts explaining the Enriquillo–Plantain Garden fault zone, which had slipped and caused the 7.0 quake. Numbers, figures, stats, logistics. Aftershocks. More dead bodies. More collapsed buildings. The early reporting seemed so impersonal, so technical, so heartless. What about the Haitian people? What about their stories? How were they feeling?

I scoured Twitter to find anything that would quench my thirst for human connection. I was looking for articles, videos, some way to hear the voices of the Haitian people. I scrolled through my Twitter feed, looking for stories.

I just want to read a stream of tweets from the people of Haiti.

What are they saying?

What do they want to tell the world?

If I were there, I'd hand them a microphone.

Why don't I?

Why don't I go down to Haiti with my own microphone—a microphone in the form of a camera?

Wouldn't it be cool if the photographs were like a visual tweet?

Maybe I could ask them to write their thoughts on rubble and photograph that.

Without thinking, without even asking Shannon, I composed a tweet: "Does anybody know how I can get to Haiti?"

What am I doing?

I don't know anything about Haiti or know anyone in Haiti.

Jeremy, you haven't thought this through.

Still, I sent my tweet out into the Twitterverse. And a stranger in Haiti tweeted back: "You can come stay with me."

It only took that reply. Six words. And with the promise of free lodging from a complete stranger in a foreign country that was suffering from the worst natural disaster of its history, I bought a plane ticket. Then I told Shannon. She nodded, hugged me, didn't question whether I should go. She knew the risks, she said, but she trusted God would protect me, guide me, lead me to the right stories. This was my work, she said.

Less than a week later, I hugged Shannon and kissed Adler and Eisley on their sweet faces. Without annoyance or the slightest hint of bitterness, Shannon said she'd be waiting for me and told me to keep safe.

"Thank you for making this world a better place," she said as I grabbed my luggage. "I'll be here praying you through."

With a grateful heart and in awe of her strength and resolve, I boarded a plane for a ten-day trip to Haiti.

Frederic Dupoux was the new Haitian friend who'd responded to my tweet, and he met me at the airport, holding a sign with my name on it. He was about my age, and despite the turmoil of his country, he smiled, shook my hand, and welcomed me to Haiti. As we walked to the car, he told me we'd stay at his family's home, that there'd been some minor structural damage, but it would be plenty safe and there was more than enough room. What's more, he said he'd stick with me for those ten days as my translator, chauffeur, and photographic assistant. Whatever it took to get the voices of the people out, he said.

We drove directly to Fredo's family's house. He said that both his parents were architects, and they'd built their home on an enormous rock to give it a firmer foundation. That decision had paid off. They were among the lucky few whose home was still standing. We walked through the front door, and his mother met us in the entry, arms open wide, as the rest of his family set food out on the table.

"You're hungry?" she asked, and without giving me an opportunity to respond, led me to the table.

After a night of fidgety sleep, Fredo and I woke bright and early and drove to downtown Port-au-Prince. When we turned a corner and the city came into full view, I saw what can only be described as the scene from a Hollywood war film. It was as if a hundred bombs had dropped on the city—maybe a thousand. What had once been office buildings, shopping markets, and residential apartments were now piles of concrete and stone. What had been homes were mounds of glass, trash, and wood. The air was hazy, thick with floating dust, sand that hadn't settled, and smoke from a thousand fires. I saw downed electrical lines, flattened cars, and hundreds of Haitians digging through rubble. Even more were simply wandering, eyes glazed over, walking to who knew where.

God, where are You in all of this?

We parked and started walking. We climbed the rubble, each step deliberate so as not to step on a nail or a shard of aluminum roofing or a body part. Bodies were piled up on the sides of the roads, nameless and unclaimed. Mothers ran through the wreckage, calling their children's names. Fathers sat, backs slumped, crying. Medical workers tended to those they could. A priest dug through the rubble with a family, searching.

The scene was more horrific than I'd expected, the suffering more palpable. Had I been overzealous in coming down to photograph the people? Was I callous to their pain, their suffering? Did they really need my camera? I must have asked some of these questions out loud, because Fredo told me I had to press on. The people of Haiti needed to be heard. Even as I choked back emotion, he assured me that we'd find the right people, the right stories. Somehow.

He spoke to a Haitian couple as they walked by, tried to draw them into conversation. They didn't want to speak to more journalists, more reporters, more photographers, they said. It had only been a few days since the earthquake, and already they wanted the foreigners to go home.

I've made a mistake. Maybe I ought to pack it up.

But Fredo was undaunted, and he assured the couple we weren't like the rest of the journalists. We didn't want to make this about our own experience. We wanted to capture their voices, their stories, to share their experiences unfiltered with the world. He worked his magic, and as he spoke, their faces softened, small smiles curling the edges of their mouths. They could share whatever they wanted? Unfiltered? And as Fredo assured them they could, what had been apprehension turned to appreciation. They were ready.

We passed them markers and picked up a piece of rubble for them to write on.

"What message do you want to send the world?"

As the woman wrote, she said she'd worked as a housekeeper until the house of her employer fell down and the owners left Haiti. Now she had no way to earn a living except to try to sell homemade candy, which she carried in a large basket. But who wanted candy in the aftermath of such an event? We did, Fredo said, and we bought more than our fair share. And while we sorted through her basket, she finished her message, written in Haitian Creole on a piece of broken stucco. *"Bondye montre chemen lespwa"*—"God, show me the path of hope." I stepped back, asked her to hold it up, and took the photograph.

Hope? I wanted it for her too, but my stomach was empty of any hope. I clenched my teeth as I silently prayed for all the things I wanted for her. Peace. Stability. Fortitude. Gainful employment. A God who would somehow undo all this destruction.

We continued walking, Fredo striking up conversations with the locals. We came to a young boy who was washing his bike in a puddle of water, and we stopped to speak with him. An older gentleman walked by and yelled, "Why are you talking to the children? They have nothing to say!" The kid looked up at the man, grabbed a marker from Fredo, and wrote his message down on a strip of wood. *"M'ta espere sa pa janm rive ankò twop moun mouri!"*—"I hope this never happens again. Too many people died."

We met a woman who told us she was a mother to seventy girls, which is to say she was the sole caretaker in the orphanage where the girls lived, the woman they called Mammie. Her heart was beyond broken when she spoke to us privately. The children were devastated; the country was in ruins. They were scrounging for food, for day-to-day provision, and where would it come from? The United States? The rest of the world? How long would that take? She muscled the questions out, tears rolling down her chiseled jaw, but when she led us to the room where the girls were sitting, waiting for a meal, she showed such awe-inspiring strength and courage. With forty girls gathered around her, she wrote her message on a piece of pink paper in French: *"Bon dieu d'onne aux enfants d'Haiti une milleure vie"*—"God give the children of Haiti a better life."

On the second day of shooting, we met a young man named Christian, who was sitting on a pile of rocks and dirt where a building had once stood. He shared his story of searching the rubble of buildings for seven days, looking for his older sister. Just as he was about to give up, he found her, her limp body being carried to the dump by a relief worker. He stopped the man, saying, "Hey! She's not trash. She's my sister." He took his sister home and buried her in what used to be their front yard. Sitting on top of that dirt mound, he wrote his message on a piece of wood: *"Mwen pa pi bon pase li!"*—"I am not better than her."

We collected and collected and collected stories, each as gut-wrenching as the last, and as I documented the messages, the sorrow set in. Every pile of rubble, every crying mother, every group of people staring blankly at what used to be a school or a doctor's office or a church—I felt the weight of it all. But there were moments of hope and resilience too. We'd caught wind of a couple who'd had a wedding planned for months. Despite the earthquake, they had decided to go through with it. Why? Fredo and I had to know. And so we made our way to the wedding venue, a church on the other side of town.

Arriving at the location of the church, we found the shell of what used to be a building—a couple of standing walls, no roof, the rest of the structure collapsed. That's where we found them, standing right next to one of the collapsed walls. They'd just said their vows, having just been united in holy matrimony in the middle of such unholy devastation. They'd lost many of their relatives in the earthquake, they said, and so many of their friends were scattered across the city. There were only a few witnesses to their most joyous day, but that small crowd radiated with the joy of hundreds, and what was still such a place of destruction was transformed into a place of pure love, if only for a moment. We asked the bride and groom what they wanted to say to the world, and without hesitation, they wrote in English on a white paper plate: "Love conquers all."

I was speechless. Humbled. Inspired. They could have postponed the wedding and sat in their suffering, too overcome with anger or sorrow to move forward. But instead they chose to celebrate the fact that they still had each other. They still had the support of loved ones. They still had light with which to see each other while they exchanged their vows, thanks to a fire someone had kindled on the street corner.

It wasn't that they went through with the wedding despite the devastation; they went through with it *because* of the devastation. It was a sheer act of hope, and, even if just for an evening, it helped to lighten the load of grief their community was carrying. That I was carrying as well.

Shooting the portrait of those newlyweds was the perfect visual representation of my experience in Haiti. Among the heartbroken, the wounded, the homeless, the desperate, and the lost, there was an undercurrent of hope. In the presence of extreme hardship, there was a sense of fortitude.

Before I left I asked Fredo if he planned on joining the growing crowd of Haitians seeking refuge outside the country. "Never," he said. "I am the future of Haiti. I have to rebuild this place for my children. This is our future."

The last picture I took was of him holding a broken laptop where he had written, "The future is in our hands." I thanked him, boarded a plane, and headed home.

Back in the States, I cataloged the photos. As I organized them, I relived the moment each was taken. The sorrow that hung in the air like concrete dust. The dreams buried under the weight of the destruction. The unfairness of it all.

What could I do with the photos? How could the voices of Haiti speak loudest? I didn't want to just share them in a blog post. I knew that the words and images of those brave Haitians would get lost, that people would simply read and then forget it. So I decided to release one image a day for seventy days on social media as part of an extended photo essay I called *Voices of Haiti*. The social media experiment caught on, gained traction, and more and more people started following along, inspired by the messages penned by the Haitian people.

Six weeks after I returned from Haiti, I received a call from Oxfam International. There was an upcoming gathering of world leaders, politicians, and international donors at the United Nations building in New York City. The goal of the meeting was to discuss and pledge funds toward the reconstruction of Haiti. The folks at Oxfam had followed my photo essay, and they asked if they could print those photos and display them in the halls of the UN to provide inspiration as attendees walked into the meeting. I agreed, and I sent the raw images over to the representatives.

The special council convened, and as world leaders walked into the meeting hall, they were flanked by oversized prints of the *Voices of Haiti*. They read the translated messages written on rubble, on broken stucco, on paper plates:

"We're afraid of the rain."
"Oh, the things I've seen."
"Love conquers all."

The leaders who met that day pledged $10 billion to reconstruct Haiti. And though I have no way of knowing just how my photos affected them, I know one thing for certain: they heard the voices of the Haitian people.

Among the most important advice I give to my fellow creators and entrepreneurs is this: see the gaps, the holes, the missed opportunities, especially in times of need or crisis. Then do something about it.

How do you identify the gaps and the holes? Often it's through frustration. A story isn't told the way you'd like. A product doesn't have a feature you need. People are being treated less like people and more like objects. Frustration, frustration, frustration. If you listen to those frustrations, if you turn your creative energy to what might fix those frustrations, the possibilities you discover might surprise you.

Some of the most important work I've done has been born out of frustration. Watching the coverage of the Haiti earthquake, I saw the gap, the hole. The news outlets were speaking for the Haitians instead of allowing the Haitians to speak for themselves—at least that's the way I saw it. Reporters, photographers, and videographers were too busy sensationalizing the destruction, and, as I watched, my sense of frustration growing, I saw the need.

Some may say that frustration isn't a good enough motivator, that it can lead people to take uncalculated risks. And I guess those folks are right to some extent. In my growing frustration over the lack of human stories coming out of Haiti, did I calculate the craziness of the situation on the ground? The potential danger of the situation? The emotional impact it would have on me? Probably not. But as the idea for elevating the human stories set in, I knew I had to try to make a difference. I knew my photography could affect the lives of the people telling the stories, the lives of those hearing them, and my life too. I knew because I knew the power of images, the power of art.

Frustration led me off the couch and into action. It gave me the motivation to push through any potential fear. It moved me to get involved in a real and tangible way, and that involvement changed me. It changed the way I viewed photography, the ways in which images and the written word could be blended to make an impact. It changed the way I saw the Haitian people—the strength, resilience, and hope they displayed in their darkest hour. Ultimately, it would change my family too.

In the months that followed, Shannon reminded me of a phone call we'd shared in Haiti.

"Do you remember when you called me from Haiti and said, 'I think our lives are about to change'?"

"Yes," I said.

"Maybe we really need to follow that. Maybe it's time to adopt."

It was our first conversation about adopting from Haiti, one that led to us starting our adoption journey in 2012. And on May 21, 2015, that journey reached its joy-filled crescendo. That was the day Ebbe and Eli, two Haitian children who'd been raised in the same orphanage, entered our lives. That was the day the Cowart family became complete.

SEE THE GAPS,
THE HOLES,
THE MISSED
OPPORTUNITIES,
ESPECIALLY IN
TIMES OF NEED
OR CRISIS. THEN
DO SOMETHING
ABOUT IT.

PORTRAIT of Christ

ORIGINAL thom YORKE drawing

Screenshots FROM the ORIGINAL
I'M POSSIBLE VIDEO

THE ACCIDENTAL
LAUNCH OF A
SPEAKING CAREER

MIKE   BEN   DAD   MOM   ME

actual test results 😞

Standard Test		LOW	AVERAGE
Convergent Thinking			
Inductive Reasoning	15		
Analytical Reasoning	5		
Spatial			
Structural Visualization	15		
Wiggly Bit	5		
Memory			
Memory for Design	25		
Observ...	15		
Knowledge		LOW	AVERAGE
English Vocabulary	5		
Mathematics			

NYC DRAWING THAT IMPRESSED MY PARENTS AT MY 7TH GRADE

NEW YORK

NOT GOOD at piano

MY Bedroom walls in 8th grade

HIGH school ART show

Bulls game 1990

MIKE

Benji   ME

MICHAEL W. SMITH

MIKE   Ben   me

that time we played the Grand Ole Opry

threefold cord

First album cover   the 615

5x5 foot painting I made for
Shannon called "one angels flight"

1st shoot in NYC w/ Steven Delopolous & my
3 megapixel Canon G1

w/ Jeremy Pinnix 2004

w/ Jimmy Abegg
2018

US in 2018

EBBE

ADLER

ELI

EISLEY

our house 2006 ?

WEDDING 1999

1st date 1996

HELP-PORTRAIT

First Event ever

FOUNDING TEAM

ANNIE   KYLE   LORI

After the 7.0 earthquake rocked Haiti on January 12th of this year, I was deeply moved as most of you were. For days I watched as the television flashed images of gloom and doom... dead ... crumbled buildings... It felt like a heartless display of numbers and statistics. "How were the people feeling?" I wondered. I was tired of heartless reports from strangers that just arrived to this devastated nation. So I decided to go to the source myself and ask them directly. My question was simply "What do you have to say about all this?" This photo essay reveals the many answers to that question.

VOICES of HAITI

the wedding

Follow the whispers,
Push past the nerves,
muster the guts, and put
yourself OUT
———— There!
Don't be afraid to be
told NO. What's the
worst that can happen.

make your STING
moment

STING

Voices of Reconciliation

"Love is the weapon that kills all evil"

"brothers in forgiveness"

"Forgiveness releases fear"

"Forgiveness is our greatest accomplishment"

"truth is freedom"

"Shared past, shared future."

"we are all Rwandan"

"still best friends"

dRones and a mattress

LOST IN YOUR SLEEP

My moment w/ santa claus

why can't my idea turn into one of these stories?

You HAVE to speak your dreams into existance.

If "I" can do all this then just imagine what YOU can do.

What have you been too afraid to try??

What voices have kept you from reaching potential?

What voices have closed your sense of wonder?

If you're alive... If you're breathing...

We need you. We need your vision.

You can do ANYTHING through Christ who strengthens you.

Chapter 10

FAILING UP

If you learn from a defeat, you haven't really lost.

–ZIG ZIGLAR

There were dozens of windows open on my Mac symbolizing all the rabbit holes I'd fallen down in the last few hours. It all started with my Google search for "how to create an app," which eventually led to things like "entity relation diagrams for beginners" and "Objective-C vs. Xcode vs. Cocoa" and "parsing and generating JSON data." So much of it was gibberish to me, and I was running in circles, but I couldn't pull myself away. I couldn't quit researching, couldn't stop trying to learn this foreign language.

The idea had come to me like so many others—out of the blue. Groggy and half-awake, I was sitting at my kitchen table with my morning cup of coffee, scrolling through Twitter and Facebook. A photo of kids running through sprinklers. A date-night selfie.

A sunset. The perfect meal. Full coffee cups. Empty wine glasses. As I browsed through the digital lives of my friends, it dawned on me that everyone seemed to post the same types of pictures. It was a trend I'd noticed before, one I'd even fallen victim to myself. In fact, hadn't I experienced a creative block lately? Hadn't I been using the same techniques?

Oh no . . . is creative block becoming an epidemic?

Has it infected me?

Coffee finished, I dressed, got in the car, and headed across town to the dentist's office. The questions followed me as I stepped through the double doors at the office, still bothered by this collective creative virus. What was the cure?

I guess I checked in, though I'm not exactly sure because I was following the questions deeper into Jeremyland. I sat in a chair (or was it a bench?), grabbed a magazine (or was it a coffee-table book?), and flipped through the pages. I turned to a photo of a staircase taken from the top down. Would I have shot it that way?

If someone told me to take a picture of a staircase, I might try shooting it from the bottom up. I don't see too many people approaching staircases from that angle.

Better yet, what if I shot it from the side and only showed a couple of stairs? What if I made the handrail the focus?

How many angles are there to a staircase, angles I'd never think to shoot?

I guess the dentist worked on my teeth, because an hour or so later I was walking out of his office, still thinking about ways to spur photographic creativity. How many different ways could you shoot a set of stairs? A coffee cup? A selfie? A date night? What if people were encouraged to see things from different points of view?

All day I scrolled through social media, clicked through websites, scrolled my Facebook feed. I lost myself in the web of images, so many of which were similar. But I found some unique photos, too, and those photos spurred new creative ideas, new things I wanted to try on my next shoot.

When I finally looked up, it was three o'clock. Wasn't I supposed to be somewhere?

My workshop!

I sped across town to my studio and walked in a few minutes late to the workshop I was teaching on portrait studio lighting. (By this point, I knew how to use a C-stand.) I took the students through the material, taught them some tricks of the trade. Near the end one of the students asked, "How do you know what to tell your subjects? About which poses to do and stuff?"

Still more than a little distracted from my daylong brainstorm, I muddled through an answer. In the end, I told him to study great portraits, see what made for great compositions. But how would he know which portraits were considered great? How would he know the right angles, the right lighting techniques, the right ways to pose his clients?

Good question.

There should be something for that.

Like a list of great portraits or examples of go-to poses or examples of good lighting techniques.

There should be some sort of tool to inspire photographers to break away from the ordinary and create the extraordinary.

The next morning I broke my routine. I stepped into the shower before my coffee and social-media-scrolling session. And under that showerhead, the place I'd had so many great ideas, another one came to me. The three separate threads from the day before—the issue of unoriginal photography, the value of unique perspectives, and the need for an idea bank—came together, fused into a fantastic solution-based idea.

I should create a photography app that provides prompts to break creative blocks.

Prompt: Find an object that looks like a face.

Prompt: Capture the genuine smile of a loved one.

Prompt: Take a photo of nature that also represents the way you feel.

The prompt could suggest angles or times of day or camera settings.

Everyone could use the same prompt but put a unique and creative spin on it.

Photographers could learn from other photographers, and they could learn by stepping outside the constraints of their own imaginations.

I jumped out of the shower, and since Shannon was out of town with the kids, I grabbed my iPhone, opened my Evernote app, and typed my explosion of thoughts. I could hardly keep up. Throughout the day I kept Evernote open and jotted down the ideas as they came to me. By the time I put my head on my pillow that night, I knew I had it—the next killer app.

Days later I met with a few friends and shared the vision. "Imagine an app that could help photographers get out of their creative rut, an app that would provide photographic tips and prompts," I said. "Simple prompts, like 'shoot a natural-light portrait of someone indoors' or 'take a photo of your shoes.' We could have more advanced prompts, too, like 'defy gravity' or 'stumble upon joy.'"

I let the concept sink in, then continued, suggesting that we could allow users to add prompts, which would make the platform more connection based and community driven. Users could inspire their friends, their followers. They could issue challenges to each other.

"I'd love for one of my friends to say, 'Okay, do this' and then I'd go shoot a photo of something I wouldn't have otherwise shot," I said.

Okay, do this.

It felt like lightning had come through the roof.

"OKDOTHIS," I repeated. What a name for an app!

That's how I found myself sucked into the world of app development. That's how I found myself with all those browser windows open. That's how I found myself reading articles about app building, trying to learn all I could. And if there's anything I should have learned from that initial Google search, it was that this project was going to be full of rabbit holes, holes that required a depth of knowledge I simply didn't have. I could come up with prompts all day long, but I didn't know how to deliver those prompts to the users.

I started working my network and was introduced to the most brilliant team of developers at a local agency that specialized in creating mobile apps. They had experience, insight, agility, and heart, and they were fluent in SDK, UX, SUP, CMS, MVP, LMNOP, EIEIO, and every other possible acronym. If OKDOTHIS was a puzzle, they were the corner pieces and edges. They could give structure to the idea.

We jumped in together and assessed the architecture of the project. OKDOTHIS would be an idea-generation community for photographers. Each photographer would give and receive prompts called DOs. We could provide an initial set of default DOs, but users would be encouraged to create their own. They'd have access to custom tools to optimize their shots—tools like ratio options, cropping, hues, and filters to help them improve their photography. Users could offer feedback to each other and maybe even some constructive criticism, but critique was not the goal. The app needed to scream community, not competition. It needed to be centered around providing growth and inspiration.

Ready, set, launch. Right?

Wrong.

We mapped ideas, user flows, and community-building tools. The team spent thousands of hours writing code, beta testing, fixing bugs. There were so many iterations, development certificates, and provisioning profiles. And four years later (we estimated it would take only six to nine months), after all that work, we finally submitted our app to the Apple App Store.

Launch day came, and we watched as OKDOTHIS went live. We figured we'd have a couple of hundred downloads from friends and family members who were cheering us on and that we'd experience slow but steady growth after launch. That's not what happened. Instead the app rocketed out of the gates and shot to the top of the App Store downloads. On launch day it became the third most downloaded app, pulling ahead of Angry Birds and the Duck Dynasty app.

Number three. Surely it couldn't get much better than that.

Until it did.

Early the next morning, I received a Facebook message from Pete Cashmore, the CEO and founder of Mashable, the web-based media platform. *The* Pete Cashmore, the man who sat at the intersection of technology and social media, the man who'd created an online platform that was the primary source for millions of monthly visitors who followed all things tech, digital culture, and entertainment. He wanted to call me. In an hour.

"You've done it," he said. "I've been brainstorming how to combine community and creativity for years, and you've done it. I think OKDOTHIS can be the next Reddit. It should be the new homepage of the internet."

I don't remember my response. It's likely I just sat there in disbelief, having forgotten how to form words. He wanted to meet and talk further, he said. The app could be the future of social media, he said. "I could possibly be interested in buying it if you're interested in selling it," he said. I bobbed my head in an up-and-down motion as if to say "yes" and "thank you" and "I can't wait to become BFFs."

I hung up the phone and called a conference to share the good news with the team. And while they were floored and flattered, they didn't think it was our golden ticket. We needed to wait it out, they said.

But it's Pete Cashmore.

"We just launched the app," they said.

Think of where he could take it.

"There'll be so many more companies trying to acquire us," they said.

You can't tell me that creating a bidding war is as important as having someone like Pete behind it.

Ultimately, I caved. My partners knew the app world far better than I did, and they were persuasive. It was still early in the game.

We owed it to ourselves to let the app flourish, to attract users to the community. We hadn't worked this hard to just hand it over to one of the biggest influencers and innovators in the social media space.

Right?

Even now I'm trying to convince myself it was the right thing to do.

As the months passed, OKDOTHIS lost steam. The community of users we had built loved it, and we even ended up releasing several updated versions that were well received. But after a while, we felt we'd taken it as far as we could. We sold it for a paltry sum. I bought it back sometime later for an even smaller sum. But it was obvious the app was going nowhere, so I killed it.

Did we fail? It looks that way.

Did that make us failures? Not a chance.

The experience of developing OKDOTHIS was one of the most fruitful of my career—an odd statement, considering the app was a blistering failure. I didn't make millions of dollars, didn't receive invites to hobnob with Silicon Valley elites, wasn't featured on the cover of *Fast Company*. In fact, the app, the community, the idea eventually met a dead end. So how was it fruitful?

OKDOTHIS had been born from a creative instinct. I'd followed those instincts and collaborated with an incredible team to bring those instincts to life. The initial launch had been impressive, so impressive that a personal hero approached me about buying it. And though my instincts had said we should sell to him, I hadn't followed them, hadn't pressed the issue with my partners. That one decision might have been the downfall of OKDOTHIS.

There's a difference between ideas that fail and being a failure. If you're a creator, you'll suffer a failing idea or two—or more—before it's all over. But those failures might be the most helpful experiences in your career. If you learn from them, if you mine the lessons and vow to never make the same mistake twice, you'll never *be* a failure. In fact, it's the collection of those lessons that brings true knowledge, true wisdom.

I'm grateful for the OKDOTHIS journey. It was a big project, one that taught me I could pull off large-scale projects. It taught me to follow my creative intuition and to follow my instincts, even when it cut against conventional wisdom or the advice of others. (It taught me to pay more attention the next time Pete Cashmore calls too.) And I'd follow that creative intuition into the bigger projects, more collaboration, and ultimately into the biggest possibility of my life.

THERE'S A DIFFERENCE BETWEEN IDEAS THAT FAIL AND BEING A FAILURE.

Chapter 11

THE ART OF FORGIVENESS

Even if they sin against you seven times in a
day and seven times come back to you saying,
"I repent," you must forgive them.

–JESUS

I was sitting on the stage at an event hosted by Catalyst, a leadership conference designed to empower young Christian leaders. I'd been asked to sit on the afternoon panel discussing how to use creativity for social good, and as I looked at the heavy hitters on that stage, I wondered how I'd been chosen.

One by one, my fellow panelists told about their work, and I half paid attention while mentally preparing to share about my *Voices of Haiti* photo series. Just before it was my turn, Laura

Waters Hinson, a woman I didn't know, launched into her story. Her opening sentence jerked me out of Jeremyland.

"Could you forgive a person who murdered your family?" she asked.

Say what?

I looked at the program notes and noticed she was the film-maker behind an Academy Award–winning student documentary about two Rwandan women who came face-to-face with the men who had slaughtered their families during the 1994 genocide. The film, *As We Forgive,* had followed those two women on their journey toward reconciliation. That day on the panel, Laura spared no detail as she described the violence of the genocide, the terror of the women. But she also shared about the beauty of forgiveness and how it was changing their community, their country.

As she spoke, I was transfixed. I wondered how I'd been so blissfully unaware of the violence on the other side of the world in 1994—especially when I had actually traveled to that country a decade later. But as I listened, I learned.

Between April and July of 1994, ethnic tensions exploded in Rwanda, and nearly one million members of the Tutsi tribe were murdered by members of the Hutu tribe. Nine years later, in 2003, due to an enormous backlog of court cases, the Rwandan government sent more than fifty thousand genocide perpetrators back into the very communities they had helped destroy. In order to be allowed to reintegrate into society, the perpetrators were asked to admit guilt to their neighbors in a community trial called the Gacaca court (loosely translated as "justice among the grass," after the grassy outdoor space where the trials used to be held). The community then decided exactly what punishment they'd mete out.

Understandably, the survivors of the genocide—a genocide that had taken the lives of one in every eight Rwandans—were racked with grief. Laura wondered aloud how it must have felt to them when the perpetrators of those genocides were allowed to move next door to some of their victims' families. Where was the justice in that? But in an effort to eliminate retribution (and all-out mayhem), the Rwandan government asked surviving Tutsis to try to seek a different sort of justice—justice that restored. The government asked the Tutsis to offer reconciliation, to extend forgiveness to those who had committed some of the most heinous crimes in modern history.

Laura showed footage from her film and shared how she cofounded the As We Forgive Rwanda Initiative (AWF-RI), a Rwandan-led organization helping to facilitate reconciliation through workshops, participatory activities, and prayer. Additionally, AWF-RI had set up dozens of As We Forgive associations across Rwanda, groups that went to public schools, prisons, churches, and villages to lead offenders toward repentance and victims toward forgiveness.

Hold up. Forgiveness is actually taking place?

Could I forgive a person who murdered my family?

Could I be their neighbor?

Laura stood tall, her words heavy with hope. I looked out at the crowd, all leaning forward, some crying. The work of forgiveness had silenced them.

That's when the spark came.

I would love to hear what these Rwandans have to say about their radical grace.

I'd love to use my camera to share these stories of forgiveness.

To do something like what I did in Haiti, but in Rwanda. Show the offender and the victim standing next to each other, maybe where the crimes took place.

Imagine what a testament that could be for people all around the world.

I stumbled through my portion of the presentation, still thinking about Rwanda. When our panel was dismissed, not only did I corner Laura backstage after the panel, but I might have behaved a little like a raving lunatic as I pitched an idea on the spot. I asked if she'd take me to Rwanda and partner with me in telling the stories of those who had reconciled and were living life together peacefully in the same community. We'd share the unfathomable accounts of suffering and atonement through photography, I said. We'd build on her remarkable work and continue to show proof of the redemptive power of forgiveness.

She said yes, and a few months later, we were on a plane headed for Rwanda.

Laura had connections and relationships on the ground, so after we landed we were taken directly to a cinder block compound surrounded by stone walls topped with broken shards of glass. We were ushered inside by a cook and a security guard. Then the family inside greeted us, and just as it'd been in Haiti, they welcomed us to a table spread with food. This was the Rwandan way, Laura said. Hospitable.

The next morning I followed Laura as she tracked down some of those affected by the 1994 genocide. Time and time again, she asked both perpetrators and victims if they'd be willing to share their stories with me and if they'd write a joint statement on an object they found at the scene of the crime. Not a single person said no. And after they shared their stories, they wrote their declarations and held them up as I took their portraits.

How I kept from breaking down during those portrait sessions, I still don't know. I gritted my teeth and clenched my jaw as I saw victims shaking hands with, hugging, and smiling at those who had killed their family members.

How?

The first two men Laura introduced me to were both in their thirties, and both wore welcoming smiles. She told me the story—how the slightly taller one with the broader smile but smaller laugh had murdered five people during the genocide. His name was Innocent, which was not his birth name. This new name had been given to him by the community after he served a few years in prison, time imposed by his Gacaca. One of the five people Innocent had killed was the older brother of Gasperd, the man standing next to him. The place where they stood was the exact spot where the murder of Gasperd's brother had taken place.

After serving his time, Innocent had made his way back to the community and found Gasperd. He'd begged for Gasperd's forgiveness during a reconciliation workshop hosted by AWF-RI, and Gasperd had extended it, releasing Innocent from the weight of all that guilt. But Gasperd hadn't just forgiven Innocent; he'd also welcomed him into an agricultural association (an ingenious effort to encourage reconciliation and alleviate poverty at the same time). Innocent and Gasperd were now dependent on each other for their daily needs.

I asked Gasperd what he wanted to say about forgiveness and reconciliation. He smiled, turned to Innocent, and the two had a brief conversation. Then they each took a white paint marker and wrote a joint message on their arms: "Love is the weapon that destroys all evil."

Innocent and Gasperd left our little place on the street, and as I watched them walk away, I couldn't keep it together any longer. I buried my face in my hands and told Laura I needed a minute. I walked down the street, considering the kind of forgiveness that could turn a murderer into a friend.

I was a lifelong and devoted Christian. I'd heard the preachers remind me to love my neighbor and to forgive others as God had forgiven me. But I'd never heard anyone at my church discuss the idea of forgiving killers. In fact, the churches I'd been in often promoted the exact opposite, advocating for lifetime incarceration or the death penalty. Some preachers I'd heard went so far as to call those things biblical. But now all those teachings rang hollow. Couldn't I learn something about forgiveness from Gasperd? Couldn't the American church?

The next morning, standing between two crumbling red mud brick houses, I met sixty-year-old Kaytani Senyana. He'd lost twenty-five members of his family during the genocide, including his wife and seven children. Next to him was Jean de Dieu Twizeremana, twenty years his junior and responsible for killing one of Kaytani's brothers. From prison, Jean had written to Kaytani and asked for forgiveness, and now they stood side by side, holding the trunk of a thin tree with remnants of the roots still attached. Written on that trunk in white paint was a simple phrase: "Brothers in forgiveness."

What would possess a killer, a man who had once believed in his own ethnic superiority, to humble himself and ask forgiveness from the family of one of his victims? What would possess a man whose family had been wiped out to extend forgiveness? Even if he could extend forgiveness in word and intention, how could he physically stand beside the man who'd tried to erase his family name?

Our team drove to a lake a few kilometers from the village. There on the shore, among patches of grass and struggling yellow flowers, stood Anasta Kasieri and Jean Claude Nshizirungu. Anasta had survived the genocide by hiding in a banana tree while his entire family was chased by a mob into the lake where we now stood. The family had drowned as he watched from his perch. Jean Claude was the son of the leader of that mob. Although his father fled the country in fear, Jean Claude had taken responsibility for the actions of his father. He'd taken on the family shame, and at the Gacaca trial, Jean Claude had asked for forgiveness. Anasta told us that his Christian faith compelled him to forgive. All those years later, the two stood on the place of the killings, and on a rock, big enough that each of them had to hold a side, they wrote, "Forgiveness releases fear."

Two days in, and I was a wreck. If Haiti had taught me the power of human resilience in the worst of natural disasters, Rwanda was teaching me the power of the gospel message in the light of the worst evil man could dish out. If Haiti had shown me how simple and privileged my American lifestyle was, Rwanda was teaching me how simple and privileged my faith was. After all, I'd never had to extend forgiveness to a killer. What's more, I didn't think I could.

One meeting ran into the next, each adding another layer to the forgiveness story. Laura took us far on the outskirts of the village to an old, abandoned house. It was from that house that Rudoviko Niyongira fled in 1994 after receiving a death threat, only to return soon after to find his wife and three children had been killed. His neighbor and friend, François Nshunguyinka, had been one of the culprits in the murders, and for his part in the crimes he'd spent seven years in prison. Racked with guilt throughout his incarceration, François had asked Rudoviko for forgiveness and later started a community reconciliation organization. The men had mended their friendship, and their families now spend time together. Pictured standing shoulder to shoulder through a windowless frame in the side of the house, they held a strip of tin roof that read, "Forgiveness is our greatest accomplishment."

See, Jeremy? Forgiveness can heal entire communities.

When I met Jean Baptiste Ngendananimana and Jeremy Hakizimana, I could tell right away that they were very comfortable with each other. Jean came out of his house, which was right next door to Jeremy's, and they immediately began talking and laughing. Jean Baptiste had lost both his parents and seven siblings in the conflict and hadn't discovered until the middle of Jeremy's murder trial that Jeremy had in fact killed one of his brothers. When the truth emerged, Jean Baptiste had forgiven Jeremy, remarking that he felt such freedom in simply knowing the truth about how his brother died. They chose to write on the murder weapon, a dull silver machete, "Truth is freedom."

See, Jeremy? Outing sin and seeking reconciliation brings freedom.

It was a reunion of sorts when Laura took me to meet Chantale Umbereyimfura and John Nzabonimpa. They had both been featured in the *As We Forgive* documentary, and I could see that Laura had grown close with them during filming. Chantale, standing tall and wearing a cheerful yellow dress, told me she'd never thought she could forgive John, the close family friend who had brutally beaten her father to death. But fourteen years after the murder,

Chantale and John had agreed to attend a healing and reconciliation workshop together. And a year later, Chantale had publicly forgiven John in front of their entire community, saying that her heart had been set free. On a piece of burlap fabric with frayed edges, they wrote in black marker, "Shared past, shared future."

See, Jeremy? Ugly histories can be redeemed and humanity united through the power of forgiveness.

Halfway through my trip I met Bernard and Ernestine, who were married after the genocide, in which nearly all of Ernestine's family members were murdered. Ernestine later forgave the killers of her family and married Bernard, a Hutu, from the ethnic group that had largely perpetrated the genocide. Bernard and Ernestine had a son and held him in the portrait along with a large ficus leaf that read, "We are all Rwandan."

See, Jeremy? Forgiveness can erase the "us" and "them" distinctions.

Honore Karuranga and Jean Damascene Nsengimana had been childhood best friends when the genocide erupted. Honore's parents and five cousins had been brutally killed, and he'd later discovered that Jean Damascene had participated in the murder of his cousins. Honore had confronted Jean Damascene while in prison, and he told me, "Because I loved him very much, I wanted to forgive him. I wasn't scared of him, but worried that he would be scared of me." I took their photograph at the scene of the murder, a wooded area right next to Honore's farm, which Jean Damascene was now helping him rebuild after playing a role in its initial destruction. Written on a tree trunk that stood tall and strong between them: "Still best friends."

See, Jeremy? Forgiveness and friendship go hand in hand.

I was deeply moved, and just when I thought my heart couldn't possibly swell any more than it had in the last couple of days, I met Xavier and Ernest. Xavier Ngirumwami had survived the genocide by hiding alone in houses and forests to evade the killers. Ernest Burakigarama had been part of a group that murdered eight of Xavier's family members. But after Rwanda's season of murder was over, Ernest had admitted his guilt to the local authorities and spent thirteen years in prison, after which time Xavier extended forgiveness. For their portrait they sat on a fallen tree in front of a house where Xavier had hidden during the violence. Behind them stood two dozen children from the village, and in their hands was a piece of cardboard that said, "We restored our humanity."

See, Jeremy? The restoration of humanity runs through forgiveness.

As we rode back to the compound after the last interview on the last day, Laura told me about her conversations with so many Rwandans over the years and how some of them likened unforgiveness to the experience of having acid eat them from the inside out. She'd heard others describe it as being trapped in a prison of hatred. "For victims," she said, "forgiving their offenders is a way of setting themselves free from the chains of anger and bitterness."

What she said rang true. I'd witnessed it firsthand, watched the survivors interact with their perpetrators with an ease, a lightness, that could only come with genuine forgiveness. But it wasn't just the forgiving victims who affected me. Through my lens, I'd captured the knowing gazes of the guilty. Forgiveness had freed them of the burden that weighed them down. It had released both ends of the burden, bringing true reconciliation.

Seeing this kind of forgiveness in action was one of the greatest gifts I've ever been given. In America we often can't forgive even the guy who cut us off on the interstate or the waitress who gave us terrible service. But those I'd met in Rwanda had forgiven the people who ripped away some of the most precious things in their lives—family, security, innocence. They proved to me that forgiveness is possible, despite the severity of circumstance. It is a force that has the power to free hearts, to mend communities, and to heal an entire country.

I returned to the States knowing exactly what I needed to do with the portraits I had shot. After sharing the photos with Shannon and telling her the stories, I sorted through the images and transcribed the messages of forgiveness. I relived each interaction, and, as I did, it was as if I could feel the release of each grudge, the weightlessness my Rwandan friends must have felt compared to the burden they'd been carrying around for all those years. I tried to put myself in the shoes of both forgiver and forgiven, and I wrote vignettes to go with each photo. I compiled it all into a photo series called *Voices of Reconciliation* and published it on my website, hoping anyone who stumbled across the images would feel what I'd felt in Rwanda.

The project had been live for only a few days when CNN reached out. They were launching a new photo essay website, they said, and they wanted *Voices of Reconciliation* to launch that site. It was a humbling honor, and I agreed, hoping their platform would drive the truths that had changed me into American culture.

Within days the CNN feature went live, and not only did it launch their photo essay website, but it was also the leading international story on CNN's website. "Could You Forgive Your Family's Killer?" the headline read, and millions clicked on that headline. Through the photos and vignettes they experienced the impact of lived forgiveness and saw the work of God in the Rwandan people.

Rwanda changed my understanding of Jesus' teaching about for-giveness. It taught me how transformative it could be, how it can literally rewrite histories. It also showed me how much work I had to do in my own life, how far away I was from being able to extend this kind of forgiveness. And this kind of life change was only possible because Laura Waters Hinson was open to collaboration. She was open to sharing her resources, gifts, and talents.

In photography, writing, art, business—any endeavor really—we so often think we're playing a zero-sum game. We act as if sharing our ideas, contacts, and resources with others might somehow ele-vate them while simultaneously devaluing our own contribution.

I can't promote that photographer because she's a competitor and I'll lose business.

I can't share my ideas and talents with that artist because he'll copy my work and not give me credit.

I can't share my resources and connections because others might make a name for themselves as a result.

But life is not a zero-sum game. Sharing with others—whether contacts, resources, or even the grace of forgiveness—allows beau-tiful things to happen. Monumental things. Things that have the power to change hearts, perspectives, minds, and lives. And in our current me-first, side-versus-side culture, collaboration is more important than ever. It requires more courage too—the courage to ask even when so many might say no. It requires the courage to say yes even if the potential collaborator might take your connections, ideas, and credit. Without the courage of collaboration, we might miss out on so many beautiful possibilities.

Through collaboration I experienced the power of forgiveness firsthand, and it changed me. That collaboration did even more though. It opened me to the possibility that the world could be changed through the sharing of ideas, platforms, and resources.

In the days following, I allowed my untamed imagination to run even wilder, knowing that with the right partners, any good idea was possible. Even the wildest ideas. The most countercultural ideas. The most audacious ideas.

Ideas rich with purpose.

IN OUR CURRENT
ME-FIRST,
SIDE-VERSUS-
SIDE CULTURE,
COLLABORATION
IS MORE
IMPORTANT
THAN EVER.

Chapter 12

ART AND THE DOORWAY TO HEALING

The artwork conveyed with an incredible clarity
precisely what she wanted to say.

—EILEEN MILLER

Have you ever experienced a perfect convergence of place, time, people, opportunities, everything? This was one of those times.

I was in Dallas for a speaking engagement at WELD, a coworking space opened by my good friend Austin Mann. WELD was an office-share hub for creatives—photographers, filmmakers, graphic designers, coders, small creative teams—who rented out desks, cubicles, private offices, or on-site photography studios. It was the sort of place where inspiration, creation, and collaboration were bound to happen.

After the event I was introduced to Matthew Williams. His girlfriend, Bethany, whom he would later marry, had founded Exile International, an organization that works with former child soldiers in central and eastern Africa, and he had become involved in the organization himself. He began telling me about their work and casually mentioned they were using art therapy with those former child soldiers.

Child soldiers, did you say?

Art therapy, did you say?

And in less than a second, three streams converged. A conversation with Shannon. What I'd been learning about art therapy. The invisible children.

Just before hopping the plane to Dallas, I'd called Shannon and told her I wanted to do a project where I collaborated with children. I talked about how I'd been spending more time creating with my own kids, how drawing with them and building with them made my heart come alive. She had noticed it, too, how my face lit up when I was creating with them, how much easier it was for me to be present with them or teach them life lessons or share life stories when we were creating. It had become such an important outlet for both me and the kids, such a place of connection. Could it be a place of connection with others too?

I'd been learning more and more about art therapy, too, a form of therapy I'd dismissed for so many years. I'd experienced the therapeutic effect in my own life, but I'd chalked that up to the fact that I was a creative. I didn't realize that there was a legitimate branch of psychotherapy built around it or that it was becoming a more widely used form of therapy for children who were struggling with different types of trauma. I didn't know there was hard science behind what I'd always suspected was true—that art fosters healing in a way that few other things can.

Days before hearing about art therapy, Invisible Children, an organization run by my friend Jason Russell, had released a documentary called *Kony 2012*, which had quickly gone viral. The documentary told the story of Joseph Kony, the leader of the Lord's Resistance Army (LRA), who had been abducting children throughout many parts of Africa for the past two decades and forcing them to become child soldiers. The film called on international leaders to find the war criminal and bring him to justice.

I had learned all about Joseph Kony during my trip to Uganda years before and was grateful the documentary had sparked awareness and discussion, but I also wanted to contribute something personally to the cause. Anything.

My passion, my creativity, my desire for justice—everything aligned in a moment, all because of a casual comment. And much as had happened with Laura Waters Hinson, the insatiable urge of collaboration fixed itself in my gut. I blurted, "Can I come to Africa with you and do art therapy with the kids?"

He smiled and agreed.

I called Shannon, and she laughed in excitement. "Of course you need to go," she said.

And that was that.

A few months later, I was on a plane headed to Uganda with Matthew and Bethany, together with my team, which included Michael and my favorite assistant and dear friend Andres Martinez. We hauled over a big box holding a Cintiq 24HD Touch graphic monitor. Leading up to the trip, I'd pitched a mixed-media project to Matthew and Bethany. We'd work with the kids and ask them to draw their stories—the pains of their past and the dreams of their future—on the Cintiq using a digital pen. Through the monitor, their drawings would be captured directly in Photoshop. I'd then take photographs of these child artists, and, using a layering technique I'd used for years as a graphic designer, I'd combine their portraits and their drawings into single pieces that showed the full spectrum of each child's story. Matthew and Bethany loved the idea.

After landing in Kampala, we rattled our way down two hundred miles of dirt roads toward Lira, our final destination. We were in the middle of nowhere, hurtling down a stretch of road lined with eight-foot-tall grass when, without warning, our driver made a sharp right turn into that grass. We cut through the sea of green, and the driver gunned it, mowing down the stalks of grass in front of him.

"No road? No problem," the driver said as if reading my mind.

Minutes later we entered a clearing with several huts. After being shown to one of them, I unpacked my gear, set up my bunk, and walked back out to the clearing, where the driver was cooking a meal over an open fire. After a day of traveling, a day of anticipation, it was a feast. And when it was over, I crawled into my cot, pulled the mosquito net around me, and let the wild sounds of hyenas and distant drums sing me to sleep.

I woke early the next morning, ready to meet the children of Exile International, and within minutes we were on the road again—which is to say, off the road again. We cut through more grass fields, more places off the map, and finally pulled into the courtyard of a multibuilding school campus in the middle of an open field. I climbed out of the van, unsure of what to expect as Matthew and Bethany pointed to the various buildings—the grade school building, the building for the older students, the meeting halls. The heat was oppressive, even for someone like me, accustomed to summers in the South. We walked the fifty yards to the schoolhouse, and by the time we entered the front door, my shirt was soaked through.

Bethany walked to the front of the class, and I followed her lead. We stood by an open window, which let a hot breeze flow through, and Bethany introduced me to forty uniformed students, each looking down and fidgeting. I was going to draw with them, she explained. She passed out large white handkerchiefs and colored markers, and she asked them to draw their stories on the linen—the pains of their past and the dreams of their future.

I walked through the room as they drew. There were soldiers, bullets, and blood. There were homes on fire. There were men in uniforms holding guns. The room was quiet as the kids accessed memories of harsh experiences and articulated them through their drawings. Some of the kids paused, covered their faces, and wept. Some grimaced. Others wore blank stares.

I picked a desk and pulled up a chair. Across from me a boy named Denis had drawn a mud-brick house. Next to it lay the bodies of his father and grandparents, who had been killed by the LRA. His mother and younger siblings stood watching an LRA soldier carry a boy—Denis—away. Next to that soldier's head, a word bubble read, "Raise them well . . . one day we'll return to take them too."

I watched as he drew on. He drew himself again, but this time he was in the bush, standing over other LRA members and child soldiers. His adult self was holding medical tools, pulling something from the bodies. Bullets. Beside those bullets were the bandages he used to dress their wounds, and next to the bandages lay the dead bodies of those he hadn't been able to save.

"You were the doctor?" I asked.

"Yes," he said without looking up, still drawing.

"How old were you?"

"Ten."

I thanked him and told him to keep going. I turned to the girl next to him, who had drawn her own nightmare. She was standing over her mother, whom she'd been forced to murder. I pointed to the picture and asked how old she was in the picture she'd drawn. "Seven," she said.

I kept moving through the classroom, kept asking questions. Every scene was as bad as the one before. One boy drew the time the rebels had made him kill his best friend and then forced him to carry the dead body on his back for three weeks. He drew black squiggly lines coming out of his own head and said they were showing that he lost his mind "because of the smell."

Another girl drew flames around two bodies, the faces of those bodies covered in blue tears. She'd been forced to burn her parents alive, she said.

Yet another drew her feet as bones and blood. Next to that drawing, she drew a self-portrait that emphasized her disfigured ears, leftover damage done by the rebels.

These were the most horrific drawings I'd seen from children, and they were inspired by the most horrific stories I'd ever heard. As I looked on, I wasn't sure whether I might cry or throw up. I'd never known this kind of evil was possible.

That night, as I was in my mud hut, trying to fall asleep, still feeling queasy, I replayed the drawings I'd seen. So much red and black. So much violence. So much pain. Did those images run like a live-action reel in the kids' dreams? I prayed for strength (for them and me), but I didn't find any in the moment. The lump in my throat loosened, and I began to cry.

Lord, how could You let that happen?

Lord, save those children from those images.

Lord, thank You for my children, who are safe at home.

The next morning, over lukewarm bottles of water (where was the coffee when I needed it?), Bethany, Matthew, and I talked about the previous day. I'd done a lot of humanitarian projects by now and seen my fair share of devastation, but the pain in those pictures was different. How could men, evil though they were, force children to kill? How could they subject them to that much pain? How could they take such innocence?

Bethany and Matthew reminded me that while those drawings were horrific, our project provided a wonderful healing opportunity for these brave survivors. Some of those children hadn't been able to talk about their experiences, they said, because their stories were too painful. But through art, through something as simple as drawing, they'd been able to express their pain. Sharing what had happened was a way of getting the pain out, of moving toward healing, restoration, closure, and peace. It was art therapy in action, in the field.

Sometimes healing requires a lot of hard work, they said, explaining that they talked a lot about healing with the kids. When they told me that *poza* was the closest Swahili translation for the word *heal*, I knew this was the name of our project: *The Poza*

Project. The name suggested a fitting trajectory for what we hoped to offer the kids: a doorway to healing.

After our morning debriefing, we returned to the school. I asked the kids to keep drawing. They could draw more memories if they needed, but they could draw their hopes for the future too. They could draw whatever came to mind. And as they set to work, I called some from their desks and taught them how to draw on the Cintiq. They'd never seen anything like it and were amazed by the ability to draw directly into a computer using a touch screen. They saw their digitized art, stared at it wide-eyed.

One girl, Dillish, put the finishing touches on her digital picture, stepped back, and looked at it. She looked at me, then looked back at the monitor. Then she went back to drawing, telling her story as she said, "They killed my mother right in front of us. My baby sister started crying, so they picked her up by her legs and slammed her head into a tree over and over again until she was dead." Her drawing was far too graphic for any childhood imagination, but this wasn't a scene from her imagination. This had happened.

Halfway through the drawing, she said she had messed up a little and asked if she could undo the last bit. She wanted to get it just right, she said. As I showed her how to do that on the screen, I considered her determination, her need for artistic perfection. Was it because she wanted to honor her sister, to capture the truth of her last moments on earth? Was it because this was the last time she was going to allow herself to focus on it?

After she finished her drawing, I walked around the room. There were more horrific images, but some of the students were drawing their futures. I picked a few of those students and asked them if they'd be willing to draw those futures into the computer. They followed me to the computer and waited their turns.

Judith drew her dream into the computer first. She wanted to become a psychiatric doctor, wanted to help others who had been traumatized by the LRA. Denis wanted to be a songwriter and wanted to lead the youth choir in his community. One little girl wanted to be a teacher, and another wanted to be an artist. There was no shortage of ambition among them, and all that ambition was accompanied by sunshine, hearts, puffy blue clouds, and smiling faces. It was amazing to me that despite the crushing blows their spirits had taken, their ability to dream had remained intact.

After two days of working with these kids, we moved to another school. Then another. We did the project at three different schools that week, lugging the enormous Cintiq in its beat-up and broken-down box everywhere we went. We drove and walked dozens of miles, past dozens of termite mounds, and met extraordinary teachers who welcomed us right into their classrooms. We came to know kids who were braver than we'd ever be. And best of all, we took part in their recollection and restoration. We witnessed the transformative power of art.

On the last day, we visited each of the schools once more, and, as we said good-bye to the kids, they seemed different. A little lighter. They still had a long way to go, of course, but healing had begun to set in. Later Bethany would tell me this was the first time the LRA victims, those former child soldiers, had been able to tell their own stories to the outside world. To me, the project had demonstrated something I'd experienced through my own art, something other experts knew to be true: the creative process and the healing process flow from a single source.

Back home, I looked through those students' digital files, that familiar lump rising in my throat. In those images I saw their resilience as well as their horrific trauma. I found glimpses of hope and redemption too. How could I ensure that the final products depicted all of this?

I spent days at my computer, layering their stories and their digital art on top of the portraits I had made of them. I blended the elements. Enhanced them. Moved them around. Made the faces break through the children's stories. I broke the images apart again, looked at different angles, combined them again. I added textures, patterns, filters. The end result was an abstract mixed-media piece for each of the seven children who had drawn on the monitor, a representation of each student's past, present, and future.

I sent the finished works to Exile International, and they uploaded them to their virtual marketplace. Prints could be purchased there, with all proceeds going to fund more art therapy programs.

I couldn't have known how *The Poza Project* would affect me. I only knew I wanted to partner with Exile International, work with kids, explore art therapy, and incorporate mixed media with the Cintiq. I had a few ideas of how that might happen, but I didn't realize where those ideas would lead me.

Into the heart of LRA territory? Yes.

Into some of the most emotionally brutal work I'd ever done? Yes.

But those ideas didn't just lead me into the darkness. They led me *through* it. They led to something more like healing—for the kids, for me, for those who bought the prints to help fund Exile International.

Through *The Poza Project* I came to see how our creativity, ideas, and artistic expression are more powerful than fear and violence. Why? Because while fear and violence only destroy, creativity, art, and ideas bring healing. And though I can't say exactly why this is true, I have a working theory.

Creativity, art, ideas, and healing all come from the same source—from God Himself. And this is why people of faith need to look for opportunities to express their creativity, their artistry, even in places of fear and violence. In the process, the wounded world might find just what it needs.

It might find something that looks like *poza.*

Months after *The Poza Project,* this lesson became more clear to me—and more personal. I had never been the smartest kid in the room. I was average at best. But God had given me a particular set of gifts—ideation, creativity, and an ear for story. He'd honed those gifts in me through so many different experiences—graphic design, portrait photography, photojournalism in Haiti, Rwanda, and Uganda. And looking back over the course of my life, I could see how He'd used those gifts in conjunction with others' gifts to bring life to the world.

My parents' gift of encouragement had lovingly directed me into a field where my gifts could flourish, gifts that would ultimately bring healing and restoration to the world. And because of that, I'd encourage our four kids (we brought Ebbe and Eli home from Haiti one month after *Poza*) to do the same. Shannon had supported so many ideas and sacrificed her time, energy, and career to raise our children while I traveled the world. Wasn't she my partner in bringing life too? Folks like Matthew and Bethany, Laura Waters Hinson, Kyle Chowning, Michael Moore, and so many others partnered and collaborated with me too. Without them, I wouldn't have known the healing power of art.

I saw my life as if it were a time-lapse video, saw how everything led to a point in Uganda. I could see the continuum of God's work in my life, and I came to understand my unique calling.

I was to partner with God, to follow His lead from idea to idea.

I was to partner with others to bring those ideas to reality too.

And those ideas were not for my own sake. They weren't to advance my name or to build my career. Instead, they were for the sake of others.

Those ideas were for the life of the world.

THE CREATIVE PROCESS AND THE HEALING PROCESS FLOW FROM A SINGLE SOURCE.

Chapter 13

FLYING INTO FIRE

"Pay attention, Job, and listen to me;
be silent, and I will speak."

−JOB 33:31

It'd been years since *The Poza Project*, and I was sitting in church with Shannon, listening while my pastor, Darren Whitehead, led the congregation in a prayer for the town of Gatlinburg. It was being ravaged by the worst Tennessee wildfires of the last hundred years. Thousands of acres, two thousand homes and businesses, and more than a dozen lives had been claimed by the fires. Gatlinburg was on the hearts and minds of everyone in Tennessee that week, our church included.

As we prayed, my mind drifted to my long history with Gatlinburg. As a kid, my family had vacationed there. As an adult, I had taken my family on trips there. Our kids loved the little town on the edge of the Great Smoky Mountains National Park, and Shannon and I did too. Sometimes we'd manage weekend getaways there just for the two of us. In fact, we'd done that a couple of winters before.

Funny story, that.

We'd rented a small mountaintop cabin for the weekend, and we arrived in the middle of the night to fresh snow. It was late, but the snow had blanketed Gatlinburg in romance. The cabin had a hot tub out back, so we'd set our luggage down and run to the deck in our birthday suits. I shut the door behind me as Shannon jumped into the steaming hot Jacuzzi, and as soon as I heard the latch click, I knew there was a problem. I turned back to the door and jiggled the knob. Then I turned it with two hands, hoping I was wrong. I wasn't. We were locked out of our cozy cabin.

I turned to Shannon, eyes wide, heart pounding, a chill settling into every inch of exposed skin, which meant every inch of my body. We had no clothes, no towels, no keys, no phones. She laughed. I panicked. That's when I considered the two options.

Option one: break in. I assessed the break-in situation but found that the windows were inaccessible, either because of their placement or because they were too small for either of us to shimmy through. Option one eliminated.

Option two: wake up a neighbor. Option two had its own complications. It was one o'clock in the morning. Driving in, I'd noted that the nearest neighbor was nowhere near us. Most significantly, I was stark naked, with only the front-door welcome mat to cover up with.

See you later, Shannon.

Off I went in the middle of the pitch-black night, through the snow, naked, barefoot, holding a welcome mat in front of my nether regions. Two hundred yards later, I saw a cabin with a porch light on. I made my way to the front door, which had a window in the top half. I looked through and saw two boys playing video games. I was one knock away from a mug shot.

I knocked. The boys looked over to see a stranger on the front step. In the dead of night. Naked. And they did what any innocent boys would have done in that situation. They bolted.

A woman I assumed to be their mother then came into the living room and looked through the front-door window. Her eyes grew wide.

Thank You, God, for this welcome mat.

I yelled through the glass, "My wife and I were in the hot tub and got locked out! Can you call for help?"

Her look of terror melted, and then she did what any not-so-innocent adult would have done. She broke down in hysterical laughter. She couldn't get a grip, couldn't stop laughing, even though I was freezing my butt off (literally). She finally managed a nod, and that was all I needed. I turned tail (also literally) and walked back up the mountain. I only looked back once to see her on the phone, watching my heinie disappear into the night.

I smiled in church as I relived the story. A laugh even threatened to rise up inside until I looked at the screen at the front of the church. The video of the current devastation in Gatlinburg pulled me back into the moment. When it ended, Darren took the stage and recommended that we take blankets, toiletries, and canned food to the drop-off center at church.

Do the folks in Gatlinburg really need deodorant, hand sanitizer, and food?

Of course they did, but I wondered if they might need something more. Wouldn't they want their stories heard? Wouldn't their stories be the key to connecting people to their needs? I considered it, and four words dropped into my head.

Drones and a mattress.

The words were almost audible. I opened my eyes and looked around the room, but everyone was praying again. Darren continued his prayer. Had he said it? I didn't think so, and as if to confirm the source was something more supernatural, I was pulled into a vision. As if I were floating, I looked down and saw a man lying on a white mattress, and that mattress was surrounded by the charred remains of his home. It was all so clear to me—the smoke, the heat, the contrast between the charred remains and the white mattress—and all of it was shot from the point of view of a drone.

I didn't own a drone, didn't even like them. I thought they were gimmicky, nothing more than glorified toys. But what if a drone could capture the scene in my imagination?

Darren said the closing *Amen*, and I pulled out my phone. If I'd learned anything about using art and creativity to help others, it was that collaboration was often a necessity. So I posted a message on Facebook, said I was doing a project in Gatlinburg (was I really?) and asked if anybody wanted to help. Next I composed a tweet and asked if anyone had connections for lodging, if anyone had a new white mattress they'd donate, and if anyone happened to know the mayor of Gatlinburg.

Twenty-four hours later, I had four drone operators, an unused white mattress, a free-of-charge (and unburned) cabin at Hidden Mountain Resort big enough to house my growing crew, and a message from a college friend, Martha, saying that her dad was the mayor.

Of course.

We arrived at the cabin late in the evening, and before we went to sleep, I shared my heart with my new crew. I also shared my vision of the man lying on a white mattress in the midst of the burned-out homes. Maybe we could capture portraits like that from above and use those images to share the stories of the people behind the tragedy. We'd connect each portrait to a donation platform, with all proceeds going to victims so they could rebuild their lives. The crew followed along, heads nodding, eyes watering.

After coffee and breakfast the next morning, Martha took us to meet her sister, Tess, and their father, Mayor Mike Werner. He cried as he shared the devastation of his town. He'd lost his own home in the fire, he said, but his concern was more for the people of his community. He wanted to be a comfort to them. He wanted to help *them* rebuild. He and Tess offered to take us around and connect us with folks we could photograph, and we took them up on the offer.

We visited first with Kirk Fleta, a local musician. Fleta had spent the last several years building his home by hand, but what had been a tedious labor of love was destroyed in a matter of minutes. It wasn't just his house that was reduced to ash though. He lost everything—instruments, sound system, and recording equipment. He lost family memories, including irreplaceable music recordings of his mother and grandfather. He lost his beloved Volkswagen camper bus. We placed the mattress where his VW had burned so hot it all but crumbled, and he lay down on it as our drones flew overhead and captured the scene. I watched through the back of my camera as I took that first image of Kirk on a stark white mattress against the dark ruins of everything he used to own, and it moved me to tears. It was the exact image I'd imagined in church only days before.

God, was that You who said, "Drones and a mattress"?

We said our good-byes to Kirk Fleta and followed Mayor Mike to meet Autumn Grushka and her seven-year-old daughter, Layla. They'd evacuated their home moments before flames engulfed it. Cinders fell from surrounding trees and embers smoldered on their driveway as they loaded their two dogs and whatever they could carry into the car. By the time they reached the bottom of their hill, the whole mountain was burning.

We set the mattress in the ashen and rust-colored rubble that had once been their home. It might have been the very spot of Autumn's bedroom, a place of comfort and safety only weeks ago. She crawled onto that mattress with Layla, the two curling up and facing each other. From above we took their photo, and I couldn't help but imagine Shannon curled up with our daughter on that mattress. I cried as I pressed the shutter release button.

We went from ash heap to ash heap, photographing families. We collected their stories and listened to how much they'd lost. The stories were harrowing, but none more so than Pete Thompson's. A firefighter, Pete had lost his home while on duty saving the homes of others. He told us his place had still been standing when the flames closed in on the mountain. He'd received a call during the worst of the fire, and he'd passed by his house on the way to that call. Several hours and too many calls later, he'd made his way back down the road toward his house, only to find it was gone. His wife and kids had already evacuated, and he had to call and break the news to them. It was the hardest thing he'd ever done, he said.

The crew placed the mattress in the ash, and Pete and his family climbed onto it, his fireman's jacket covering them all as a blanket. It was a stark image—a public servant who'd lost all his possessions trying to save others.

In the end, our four-day project allowed us to meet and share the stories of twenty residents. Yes, there was devastation and deep loss, but the Gatlinburg residents were resilient, hopeful, and even joyful. Time and time again they assured me they'd be fine. "We're mountain tough," they said, and it was true. Their town had burned, but the people couldn't be kept down. Their tenacity was contagious.

The night we wrapped, I drifted to sleep thinking the series might be perfect for *Time* magazine. I'd never worked with them, but it seemed like a concept and story they'd appreciate. How would I get in touch with *Time*? I didn't know, but, as it turned out, I wouldn't have to work too hard to find out. The next morning I exchanged good-byes with the crew before pulling out of town. I stopped at a diner, ordered an early lunch, and as I waited for my order I checked my e-mails on the phone. I had one unread e-mail, and it was from a photo editor at *Time*. He said he'd been following the project through my Instagram feed and wanted to build a website around the series.

Are you kidding me?

I had followed a whisper in church, and to bring that whisper to life, I'd turned to collaboration, a lesson I'd learned through the years. As a result, tens of millions of people heard the stories of twenty people from Gatlinburg through *Time* magazine. Funds were raised to help those folks rebuild their lives, and a small town in Tennessee got the world to join them in being mountain strong.

Following that whisper became a powerful testament of how we can use our creativity to serve others.

Though no one's ever said it to my face, there are some who have written me off as a crazy creative who hears voices and sees visions. Others have given me too much credit, using phrases like "creative genius."

Maybe I am crazy, and I can assure you I'm no genius. (Remember that D in college photography?) But whether I'm crazy or a genius or somewhere on the spectrum in between, I have one thing going for me: I've learned to listen to my ideas. And here's the best way I've found to describe how that process works for me:

God throws ideas at me like crumpled-up paper wads. My job? To pick up those paper wads. To flatten them out. To read the messages like a map. And to follow that map.

I've considered the analogy over the years, and the truth it represents has been incredibly freeing to me. I can't take the credit for any of my more successful ideas. In each case the idea came, seemingly from out of nowhere, and hit me upside the head. All I was responsible for, really, was responding to the idea and doing something with it.

I believe that in each case it was God—the source of all good ideas—who chose me. Why? I don't know. But if you'd like me to hazard a guess, I might say that God throws these ideas at all of us all the time. The question is whether or not we pick them up. Unfold them. Follow them.

Sitting in church, praying for the victims of the Gatlinburg fire, I had a paper-wad moment. The message on the piece of paper was simple: "Drones and a mattress." I didn't second-guess it. I didn't question it. I didn't push it away and move on to the next thing, the next event, the next cause. Instead, I acted on it. And in acting on that idea, I learned so much.

The *Voices of Gatlinburg* project taught me new things about perspective. It challenged me creatively, made me burn down the creative box that constrained so much of my photography. It deepened my understanding of the need for collaboration, too, leading me to work with experts and creatives in other fields.

As I've said, I had never considered using drones in photography. But by listening to God's whisper and by collaborating with others to capture the unique angle, I was able to add a new tool to my artistic repertoire. More important, my team and I were able to foster human connection by showing shock and grief and hardship in a new way. The contrast of the white mattress against the dark ruins. The body language of survivors as they lay together. Devastation sharing the frame with tender human connection. By sharing these kinds of images with the world, we became agents of healing.

We can ignore the paper wads thrown by God. We can pick them up, unfold them, read them, and then discard them if we find the message too confusing or overwhelming. But if we take the messages to heart, if we act on them, we might discover what it looks like to collaborate with God and others. We might find the places where creativity and empathy meet and where destruction gives way to renewal.

We might find the point where fear bends to possibility and possibility becomes purpose.

GOD THROWS
THESE IDEAS AT
ALL OF US ALL
THE TIME. THE
QUESTION IS
WHETHER OR NOT
WE PICK THEM UP.
UNFOLD THEM.
FOLLOW THEM.

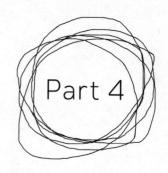

Part 4

PORTRAIT OF AN ARTIST AS A DREAMER

Chapter 14

THE ART OF PURPOSE

If your dreams do not scare you, they're not big enough.

—ELLEN JOHNSON SIRLEAF,

AFRICA'S FIRST WOMAN PRESIDENT

For the five years that Caryn was my agent, she'd been telling me that I needed to move my family out to Los Angeles because that's where all the work was. "It's always sunny and we have palm trees," she said.

I'd refused. Nashville was my home, I told her.

But after Shannon and I prayed about it for a while (approximately four years and eleven months), we had warmed to the idea. At the time, our kids were young and weren't yet in school, so uprooting them wouldn't be much of a problem. Maybe we should just try it. What could it hurt? So we found renters for our home in Nashville and moved to the Woodland Hills suburb of Los Angeles.

Caryn had been right about all of it. The sun, which always seemed to be shining. The palm trees, which were beautiful and seemed to be everywhere. And the work—was it possible that every company in the world had an office in LA? All signs pointed to yes on that one. But better than all of those things was the convenience of in-person meetings with clients. That alone was worth the cost of the move.

Living in a different state and time zone than 90 percent of my clients had made me a master of conference calls and video chats, often at dreadful hours. But now, on the West Coast, I usually opted for in-person meetings, where I could feed off the energy of my clients and they could feed off mine. Now that I lived across town from so many of the people I was working with, I could hop in the car and meet them at a moment's notice, or at least as quickly as LA traffic would allow. My productivity went through the roof.

In the first month of living in LA, I received a phone call from VSCO, the photography mobile app. I was slated to shoot promos for them later in the day, and they asked if I could head to the Standard hotel for an impromptu preproduction meeting a couple of hours before the shoot. I most definitely could. Aside from the new ease of commuting, it was a pretty standard afternoon (pun intended). Nothing out of the ordinary. No obligation. I wasn't chasing any big ideas.

What I didn't know yet was that the afternoon was going to turn out to be anything but standard, anything but ordinary.

I drove to the hotel, received a key from the front desk, hopped into the elevator, and hit the button to take me to the eighth floor.

Standard, right?

Ordinary.

The elevator doors opened, and I walked down the hallway. Because it was my first trip to the Standard, I took in all the details. And one of those details stuck out more than the others. Instead of having a simple room number on the door, each of the doors had something like an old-school name tag hanging on it.

"Hello! My Name Is 821."

"Hello! My Name Is 823."

"Hello! My Name Is 825."

I chuckled at the clever personification. But then everything in my head went tunnel vision as the ideas came and came and came.

What if each of those door name tags actually had a face and a name—and maybe a couple sentences of a story?

As you walked down the hall, you'd pass little short stories about someone.

When people traveled, they could connect to a larger story, a story that started at the door and continued in the room.

It would be cool if the story in the room was a child's story.

Maybe a child's face could be on the door too.

A child in need.

The room could be named after a child in need, and maybe fifty cents or one dollar a night could go to that specific child.

I think Compassion International does child sponsorships for, like, thirty dollars a month.

How much are the rooms here?

Surely each room could give thirty dollars a month toward a child.

I arrived at the room where the meeting was scheduled, and I looked down at the electronic hotel key I had been given. *Shouldn't the key card to the door have some connection to a physical key?* Caitlin Crosby, the founder and CEO of the Giving Keys (and the long-lost sister I never had), came to mind. Her company repurposes old keys into accessories, and each key is engraved with a word, like *Hope, Love, Dream, Create,* or *Courage.* Her customers wear those keys until they meet someone who needs the word written on that key; then they give them away. And the best part? Her company employs people transitioning out of homelessness to create the products, which gives them income and purpose.

What if all the hotel keys were Giving Keys—or at least helped promote or share the story of the Giving Keys?

Caitlin would want in on this. Wouldn't she?

I swiped the hotel key card, the green light flashed, and I entered the room. And this is where things got weird. I can't properly explain what happened next, except to say that *everything* happened next, all at once.

I saw the bed.

I know about nonprofits who make blankets and linens and pillows.

I saw the TV.

What if instead of the inevitable "adult programming," there was a list of social documentaries to watch?

I considered the Wi-Fi.

What if connecting to the internet required a five-dollar surcharge that went to free women from sex trafficking or the porn industry?

Generic corporate artwork hung on every blank wall.

So many of my friends are talented humanitarian artists and photographers. What if their original art hung on the wall, and it could actually move and inspire people? What if people could actually buy prints of that artwork to help support the artists?

I saw the mini soap.

There's that nonprofit in Nashville that helps women who've survived trafficking and addiction and teaches them how to make soaps, shampoos, bath oils, and candles.

I walked over to the table, where all the VSCO guys sat staring at me. They looked a little bewildered, which was understandable because I'm sure that my eyes were glazed over and that I looked certifiably crazy or at least drunk.

What if every single thing in the hotel created a better life for someone else?

What if every single thing served a purpose?

"You guys, I'm having an idea for a hotel right now," I said as I sat down. They gave me sideways glances but leaned forward to listen. I spilled all those ideas, and they listened to my stream-of-consciousness rundown. I shotgunned ideas at them, then said, "It'd be a sort of purposeful hotel, and every item in the hotel would tell some kind of story."

Their eyes were wide, and one pointed to his arms, said he had goose bumps. Another said it was an amazing thought, said he'd stay in a hotel like that. Another sat silent, nodding and smiling.

We couldn't sit in the idea forever, of course. We had a photo shoot to do. So they each said I should keep noodling on the idea; then we moved on and got down to business. But as you might guess, for the rest of that meeting, I was lost in Jeremyland. I did my best to remain present to the client, to drag myself into the conversation, but when my eyes invariably wandered around the room, another explosion of ideas came.

Were those curtains made in a sweatshop?

Is the stationery on the desk made from recycled material?

What if ordering room service helped feed a child in need somewhere else?

Could we dig a charity: water well like I saw in Africa in a hotel lobby?

We finished the meeting, then the shoot, and I made my way to the car, head still swimming in the pool of ideas. Miracle of miracles, I made it home without getting lost or driving the wrong way down a one-way street or running a stoplight and T-boning a city bus. And once in my driveway, I sat in the quiet, trying to slow my thoughts down enough to collect them. How on earth was I going to articulate any of this to Shannon?

There's no way she'll go for it.

It's just so big.

She'll think I'm crazy—and she'll be right.

I walked into the house and found Shannon doing dishes in the kitchen. After all those years together, she knew what the look on my face meant. She placed the sudsy baking dish she was washing back into the water-filled sink, turned to face me, and said, "Tell me about it."

I told her everything, how it all started with the "Hello My Name Is" name tag, which had led to a simple idea: "What if every room had a child's name, face, and story on it, and a portion of the room rate went toward sponsoring that child?"

Shannon put her hand on her chest and took a deep breath.

I told her how that idea led to another, the idea about partnering with the Giving Keys organization. I told her about walking into the room, about the explosion of ideas as I examined every nook.

The bedding. The social films. The soaps, towels, and artwork. Everything in the hotel could be connected to a bigger purpose, I said. And then I said something I hadn't expected.

"Maybe we have a chance to fundamentally change the hospitality industry, to fundamentally change the way people interact with global poverty."

I exited the world of my ideas and came back into the room, eyes focusing on Shannon. It had been four years since I'd told her about my Help-Portrait idea. Since then I'd shared a hundred other ideas with her. An online-education app idea. My children's photography studio franchise. A dozen TV show concepts. A traveling photography-studio truck. Augmented reality ideas. National holiday ideas (yes, holiday ideas). More app ideas. Few of those ever really connected with her, and most had been followed with something along the lines of, "Okay, can you please take out the trash? I have to run to Target." But as I studied her face now, I could see it. She got this idea, or maybe this idea got her.

She was nodding, eyes glassing over. She took a deep breath, tried to say something. She couldn't. Tears came, poured down her cheeks. Finally she gained her composure, walked to the table, and sat down. I followed her, sat beside her, and for the next thirty minutes we dreamed about what this hotel could be. What if it was a global hotel chain? What if each location in the chain supported different people, maybe people in that particular city? What if every single aspect of the hotel could help people earn a living, even the furniture? What if everything was on purpose?

What if it was called The Purpose Hotel?

The air left the room.

This is brilliant—but impossible.

There's no way.

It's too big.

I can't.

The familiar feeling of doubt came over me. There was no way that someone like me—this little artist, this absentminded photographer, this builder of only the skyscrapers in Jeremyland—could create a hotel chain. I didn't have the know-how, the business sense, the industry awareness to pull off the idea.

I didn't have to say anything. My face outed me.

"This idea is big." Shannon reached out and squeezed my hand. "It's too big to be afraid of."

She was right, of course, but that didn't fix the fear, the doubt, the fact that I had no idea how to start a hotel chain. I stared at Shannon across the table, searched her face for any signs of fear, any doubt. There were none.

"If you don't try this before you die," Shannon said, "I'll be really disappointed."

The idea haunted me for the rest of the day. The next day too. It followed me everywhere I went—to client meetings, dinner dates, the bathroom. Months later I was lying in bed, unable to sleep as ideas for The Purpose Hotel kept coming. I'd been considering the lobby, thinking through how people might be invited into purpose from the minute they stepped into it, when my cell phone lit up the corner of the room.

Who could be texting me at two o'clock in the morning?

I reached over and grabbed it, hoping there wasn't some type of emergency. The text was from an old friend of mine named Jesh de Rox, a fellow photographer in the industry. We weren't close by any means, and it had been a long time since we last chatted.

I read the text.

What the . . . ?

I read it again. Then again.

"I believe you are blessed with the vision of a spiritual architect," the text read. "May God give you the strength to build all you have in your heart."

That text had come out of nowhere, and it left me floored. Speechless. Humbled. Not only had Jesh and I rarely corresponded via text before, but the world was supposed to be sleeping. For him to feel the need to send that to me right then—or to send it at all—couldn't be a coincidence.

Could it?

I wrote him back: "Wow, man, you have no idea how accurate the words *architect* and *build* are for what I feel called to do lately. Those words are quite prophetic. Thank you for sending this note. I'll explain soon the new vision that God has given me."

The moment I pushed Send, I felt like a fraud. I wasn't going to move forward with the hotel idea, right? So why would I allude to it like that? And the last line was a flat-out lie. I'd never share the vision with him because there wasn't a vision to share. It was a nonstarter. A pipe dream.

What kind of self-employed freelance artist builds a global hotel chain?

Geez, Jeremy, go back to bed.

Maybe God was trying to send me a message. He'd spoken through the Standard, through the affirmation of my clients, through my wife, through a friend in the photography industry. But I'd already stopped listening, at least for the moment.

A month passed. Then another. Then a year. When the idea resurfaced time and time again, I pushed it back.

I couldn't possibly.

What do I know about the hospitality industry?

For three years I kept those questions—those excuses—handy. I talked myself out of believing I could do it, buried the idea, shot it down whenever it resurfaced. It was too big, too scary, and too foreign. There was too much I didn't know about—construction, investors, accounting, microeconomics, tourism management—and I couldn't just figure it out by reading *Building a Hotel from Scratch for Dummies.*

So I focused on other things. We ended up moving back to Nashville from LA (a long story centering around what *not* to do when renting out your house in Nashville, a story with so many twists and turns it might be my second book), and we officially started a grueling, rewarding, heart-wrenching adoption process (my third book). But even though there was so much keeping me busy, the idea of The Purpose Hotel kept coming up.

From time to time, Shannon asked, "When are you going to pursue the hotel?"

"Someday, maybe," I'd say, trying to sound indifferent. If I sounded like I didn't care, maybe someday I *wouldn't.*

And every time she had the same comment: "If you don't follow this idea before you die, I'll be disappointed. If you don't at least give it a chance, you'll never know the impact or opportunity missed for those in need, for those it will serve. The Lord gave you this idea on purpose. He can do this. You can do this."

No pressure.

For the majority of my life, I've nursed a healthy awareness of my fear. I've listened as fear reminded me of my limitations: *You can't jump off that cliff. You can't try out for that play. You can't set up an impromptu photo booth at the concert. Cold calls never work.* But time after time, I have refused to obey the voice of fear. In fact, I've jumped into the things my fear was warning me against. And time after time, doing the very thing I was afraid to do has led to incredible possibilities.

But in those early days of dreaming about The Purpose Hotel, the fear was simply too big, its voice too loud.

You're not smart enough to pursue a business as complicated as hotel construction and management, fear told me.

You'll make a huge mess of things, it warned.

You'll run your family into financial ruin.

There are already too many hotel chains in the world.

I allowed that fear to control me, gave it space to convince me that I wasn't the guy to reimagine the hospitality and hotel industry. Who was I to pursue something so grand? Who was I to take on that much risk, that much potential failure, especially when I already had the kind of booming photography business that most photographers dreamed of? The fear and the practical realities came head-to-head with the audacious idea that had gripped me at the Standard hotel, and the fear and practicalities almost won.

Here's the truth: no one ever created something truly spectacular, something audaciously purposeful, by giving in to fear and practicalities. Instead, the true visionaries are those who listen to the fear, examine the practical limitations, and let those things inform their plan of attack. Then, once the plan is formulated, they take the calculated leap. Those calculated leaps are what change the world.

The problem was, I wasn't prepared to make such a leap. Three years after the idea for The Purpose Hotel first hit, I still couldn't push through the fear.

Would I ever be able to?

NO ONE EVER
CREATED
SOMETHING TRULY
SPECTACULAR,
SOMETHING
AUDACIOUSLY
PURPOSEFUL,
BY GIVING IN
TO FEAR AND
PRACTICALITIES.

Chapter 15

THE ART OF LEGACY

Being the richest man in the cemetery doesn't matter to me.

—STEVE JOBS

When I was asked to speak at the 2014 Wedding and Portrait Photographers International conference in Las Vegas, I couldn't help but think of my oldest brother, Mike. The WPPI gathering is a weeklong photography expo featuring instruction from big-name photographers in the wedding and portrait world, and Mike had become quite the accomplished wedding photographer. He'd taken up photography soon after I did and had found his niche capturing love with his lens. He could tell a story with a wedding photo, and as I considered the invitation, it seemed to me that he should have been the Cowart invited to lead the session.

Come to find out, he was already booked to shoot a wedding in Hawaii and wouldn't be attending the conference at all. In fact, he was scheduled to fly to Kona on the same day I would fly to Las Vegas. And so, though we were on different sides of the airport at different gates, we texted back and forth as we waited for our flights. I boarded, and just before I set my phone to airplane mode, he texted that his flight had been canceled.

I arrived in Vegas hours later and checked in to my hotel. I made my way to the venue, walked through the exhibit hall, and stopped at a few of the booths. I made small talk with a few folks who knew my work, then made my way to the room where I was scheduled to present, where I was met by five hundred eager photographers. Wedding photographers. Portrait photographers. Graphic designers. Photography assistants. The emcee introduced me. I took the stage. And for whatever reason, I fished my phone out of my pocket and placed it on the podium. Faceup.

I started my presentation, started speaking about the importance of light. As if on cue, my phone lit up. It was a microdistraction, and as distractible as I am, it sucked me in. It was a text from my dad, and it was about Mike.

Odd.

I held a finger to the audience and read the text more closely. "911. Call us," it read. "It's about Mike." Everything slowed down, and I broke out in a cold sweat. I looked at the crowd, told them I was sorry but there was an urgent call I needed to make. I stepped offstage, called my dad, and he told me the news.

Mike was gone. He'd had a massive heart attack. He was only forty-three years old.

I told my father I'd come home as soon as I could, hung up

the phone, and stared at the audience. Everything froze. It was all silence until I stepped back to the mic.

"I'm sorry," I said. "I just received the news that my brother just passed away."

As soon as the words came spilling out, I slipped into my memories. How we'd played baseball in the backyard for years. How he'd encouraged my art, worn the T-shirt of my Michael Jordan drawing even after my party. How he and Benji and I had formed a band together. How he'd followed me into photography and carved out his own niche.

Our relationship hadn't always been easy though. We'd had our arguments, our differences, maybe like most youngest and oldest siblings do. We hadn't been all that close in my younger adult years. But in the months leading up to the WPPI conference, we'd grown so much closer.

Two months earlier, in fact, my older brothers and I had taken our daughters to a daddy-daughter dance. In my memory I saw Mike dancing with his daughter, Reese. Holding her close. Spinning her. I could see the photo I'd taken of that night, the one I'd snapped when Reese was resting her forehead on his, both of them smiling. That was the last photo I'd taken of him. In fact, it was one of the last times I'd ever seen him.

Coming out of my memory, I stared at the crowd, who were still frozen. "I have to leave," I said, and the crowd seemed to nod in agreement. I had to get home to my family.

On the flight home, my thoughts returned to the daddy-daughter dance. I replayed it moment by moment, looked at it from every angle. Was there a sign I missed? Did Mike seem to be struggling physically? If he was, I hadn't been able to tell. I only recalled how happy he'd seemed, even though he'd been put through the wringer over the previous decade.

There'd been a horrible bicycle accident in which he'd broken multiple facial bones and been blessed with more than 150 stitches. There was a painful divorce from the mother of his two kids. He'd lost a job he loved.

Somehow, though, Mike had managed to turn all those losses around. He'd come through all that grief with an incredibly strong bond with his son and daughter and a new photography career. He was the most resilient man I knew.

And then, in an instant, he was gone.

Mike was a Christian, and I knew he'd made it home. I knew he was in the place of perfect peace, perfect rest, perfect joy. But for those of us left to live without him, it was a heart-wrenching loss, one that seemed so unfair. It was unfair that my folks had to bury their son. It was unfair that his kids, Reese and Noah, were left without their dad. It was unfair that I wouldn't be able to exchange another text message with my brother or share in the joy of his photography.

I attended the visitation a few days later, and the line went out the door. The funeral was packed with folks who'd been affected by Mike's life, his joy, his larger-than-life personality. It was a somber celebration, one that was fitting, but after the funeral his friends told stories. They talked about how Mike was the life of the party, how he was always quick with a smile, a laugh, a joke. One of his friends shared that he'd give you the shirt off his back, and I remembered Mike's generosity, how he'd often buy groceries for a single mother or homeless folks or help a down-on-his-luck friend with the rent.

He was the most unique individual, the happiest, the most vivacious. Now the world was without his contribution, and we were supposed to walk away from the graveside and back into our everyday lives. We were supposed to move on without him.

Mike's death did what death does to any artist: it turned me inward. There were moments when I missed him so much I had to stop myself from texting him. I held back tears in public, but in the car or the shower or any more private place, I couldn't hold it together. My big brother, the one I'd chased in childhood, the one I played music with through college, the light of any family celebration, my colleague in photography—he was gone.

The weeks passed following Mike's death, and what had been grief turned to angst. Questions about my own mortality, my own legacy pulsed. Throbbed. Somehow every heartbeat felt tenuous. Life seemed much shorter.

I wish that epiphany—the understanding of just how brief life is—would have pushed me to take the most audacious risk. I wish the epiphany would have thrown me into exploring The Purpose Hotel. I still wasn't ready for that though. The sprawling, unwieldy idea was just too frightening. There were lessons I still needed to learn, too, though I didn't know that at the time. So instead of going all in on my biggest idea, I took a baby step in the direction of legacy.

I considered this modern age and how so much of our time is spent documenting our thoughts and our feelings on social media. What if we put that much energy into documenting our wisdom? What if Mike's kids had access to more than his daily Twitter thoughts? What if they could access his insight, hear him share the hard-fought wisdom that his individual struggles and unique experiences had given him? There was so much he didn't publicize for all the world to see. What if he had replaced tweeting with teaching?

It kept me up at night, this thought that the most important things Mike had learned in life had been lost with his passing. By extension, weren't the most important things I had learned at risk of passing away? But what if each of us could preserve our knowledge? What if that knowledge could be passed from one generation to the next?

What if my grandparents, my great-grandparents, had had access to the technological capacity we have today and had used it to document their knowledge? I'm not talking tips on better brain surgery techniques or how to analyze stock data or how to manipulate an image in Photoshop. What if they had documented just everyday stuff? What if I could watch a video of my grandfather teaching me how to change the oil or explaining what plants he grew in his garden and why? What if I could see the tools and methods he used? What wouldn't I pay to watch a video of my dad at work when he was my age, taking me through what he actually did for a living. What were his favorite parts of the job? Why?

The more I thought about it, the more captivating the idea was. The more captivating it was, the more I became obsessed with it. My obsession brought clarity.

What if we all decided to be teachers, but without the classroom setting?

What if we passed on what we're passionate about?

What if we could create an accessible database of expertise?

What if it could be about everything?

Photography? Sure.

Business skills? Yes.

Raising children? Work-life balance? Fear of failure?
Absolutely.

The following day I was preparing for a photo shoot. My assistant and I were sorting through a pile of gear, and I flashed back to my first day on the *Prison Break* set. I'd come so far from being the rookie who didn't know how to use a C-stand or a softbox. After years of working with all that equipment, though, I'd become an expert. I knew secret hacks that would create certain effects. I knew what types of gear I preferred and why. I considered the perspectives I'd gained through the years, and I knew there were photographers who would love to hear me riff on those thoughts. My perspectives, my expertise—how could I leave that as a sort of legacy?

I turned to my assistant and asked him to grab his phone and start rolling. Looking into his iPhone, I gave a few job details. We were shooting an album cover. I planned to use a particular lens for particular reasons, and I outlined those reasons. I detailed the lighting setup, showed why I'd chosen to use LED lights instead of strobe lighting. I explained my choice for the tethering kit. It only took me a couple of minutes, and it was pretty technical (the kind of stuff photography nerds might geek out about), but it was the kind of information I wished I'd had when I was on my first studio set, drowning in a sea of unfamiliar equipment.

As I rewatched the video that night, I noted the limitations. The footage wasn't top quality, and I could have articulated my choices a little better. Still, the format—part tutorial, part real talk—served as a cool way for people to collect morsels of advice from someone who had learned his craft through trial and error, organically. It would be a way to share the wisdom I'd worked hard to acquire. I wasn't so arrogant as to think my insights were extraordinary or life altering, but I knew someone might find them helpful. It was a way I could leave something for the world, or at least the photography community.

I spent the next nine months filming the ins and outs of my daily life as a professional photographer. Lighting setups. Equipment choices. Camera settings. Shooting techniques. I shared natural lighting practices, my process for retouching, and how I managed image rights. I shared outside-the-box editing techniques and shared the stories of how I'd used those techniques to create stunning portfolio images.

Images like my portrait of English singer-songwriter Imogen Heap.

I had been a huge fan of Heap for years, and once, as a young and upstart photographer, I'd messaged her on Flickr, asking if I could shoot her for my portfolio. I didn't know whether she would receive the message, let alone write me back, so you can imagine my surprise when I received her response. She'd reviewed my work, she said, and she'd love to schedule a shoot with me.

We arranged a place and time for the shoot, and I showed up with my camera, a simple lighting setup, and a white bedsheet. (In the industry we refer to this kind of setup as "super professional.") The location we chose was sparse, and one of the only items in the room was a deer head mounted on the wall. We set to work, and I took photograph after photograph, sometimes using the sheet as a backdrop, sometimes not. Well into the shoot, Imogen moved to the deer's head and put her hands on either side of its snout. I shot her profile while she basically held that deer head against the backdrop of the most terrible wallpaper I'd ever seen. We played, had fun with the camera, and at the end of the shoot, I thanked her for her time.

Back at the studio, I looked through all the images, and one stood out—the one of Imogen holding the deer head. But the deer head wasn't what made it special, and the terrible wallpaper backdrop didn't enhance it. What made that photo great was Imogen's pose. It was somehow magical, experimental, the kind of thing that embodied her music. That photo was definitely the one. But what to do about the deer head, the busy background?

I opened the photo in Photoshop and removed Imogen from the photo entirely. I pulled her into a new file, retouched her skin the slightest bit. (Oh, the power of modern technology.) Isolated against a now empty white backdrop, she looked even more magical. But how could I round out the setting?

I imported the image of a landscape I'd shot, brought in some clouds, and pushed it all behind her. I tweaked the photo for an hour or two to make sure it was neither too obvious nor too subtle. I adjusted the brightness, the color, the contrast. It was coming together, but it wasn't quite there.

That's when the idea struck.

I'd recently bought a bunch of vintage cameras on eBay, medium-format cameras with top-down viewfinders from the 1920s and 30s. What if I shot digital photos through those old cameras? What if I scanned and layered all of the images on top of each other to create a one-of-a-kind effect?

With the image up on my cinema display, I picked up each camera in turn, as if they were on a conveyor belt, and used it to take a picture of the picture. And because those old lenses had dirt, dust, and scratches on them from years of use, the resulting shots looked slightly distorted and a little dingy.

Perfect.

Except the last camera. That lens was clean, and it didn't add anything to the photo.

That won't do.

I picked up the camera, walked into my kitchen, lit some matches, and set the lens on fire. (See? Sometimes you have to hack technology, even if it's old technology.) And because I knew camera lenses, I knew enough heat on the glass would make it bubble up. I knew it wouldn't otherwise harm the camera. I also knew I would get an unparalleled result that would warp all the shots to come. And I was right. That camera's effect was my favorite out of all of them.

When I was through shooting, I sat down at my computer with all the different images of the image and got to work. I combined layer upon layer of distorted Imogen images, and with each layer, the effect became more bizarre. Noisy. Grainy. Dusty. Full of all kinds of weird textures that really brought the image to life.

I layered until I was satisfied, until I thought another tweak might ruin it all. (There's a saying I try to live by: Half of art is knowing when to start, and half is knowing when to stop.) I stepped back to look at the final image, and I couldn't help but smile. It had turned out exactly the way I'd hoped, exactly as I'd seen it inside my head, but better. It was ethereal. Otherworldly. It was just like Imogen's music, but it was a photograph.

Outside-the-box thinking always served me well. Extremism in my art always served me well. Deconstruction, setting things on fire, flipping things on their heads—these had always worked for me, and I knew they'd work for other photographers if they'd be open to learning new techniques and taking risks. I wanted to encourage that kind of risk taking, to show the upside of experimentation. I also wanted to get down to the real-life stuff of photography nobody teaches: how to break the right rules, how to be stupid bold, how to bring ideas to life. I wanted to explain the reasoning behind my artistic choices, and I wanted to encourage people to make their own choices. So I made some videos with that kind of content.

It wasn't just about photography though. I wanted to document life lessons, things I'd be proud for my kids to see one day. So I recorded videos about my life outside of photography, about my role as a husband and father, the ways I encouraged my kids to follow their own creative leanings. I shared stories of how art can play a role in healing and restoration, stories about Help-Portrait, Haiti, Rwanda, Uganda, Gatlinburg. If it was important to my life, I captured it, and then I gathered all the videos together to create what I called See University, an online vault of educational photography videos.

The next step was to upload the videos so they would be available to anyone who wanted to view them. But instead of uploading the videos onto some preexisting platform, like YouTube, I decided to create my own online platform. I worked with content strategists and developers to build a hub that housed the videos, and we included a dashboard where people could manage their accounts. For a nominal fee, anyone could sign up and access video lessons that spanned dozens of topics.

One year after Mike's unexpected death, See University launched with more than seventy-five videos. It was a tribute to my brother, a reminder that life is about more than success. It's about leaving a legacy of learning, about sharing your wisdom and experiences with the rest of the world.

The idea caught and then spread, and before long See University had more than 150 video lessons and a lot more subscribers than I was expecting. Its growth was a true testament to people's thirst for knowledge. See University also generated more consistent income than I'd ever made in my life, and I hadn't even set out to monetize it. At best, I'd hoped to defray the costs of creating the platform and hosting the videos. But there I was—little, shy, average Jeremy from Hendersonville, Tennessee—and I'd created a viable business generating great passive income.

I kept recording videos, kept posting them in See University. But two years in, I grew weary of it all. I had wanted to teach and share everything I knew about photography. I'd wanted to leave what I'd learned in a format that would outlast me. But as the platform grew, so did the demands. People wanted new material, more and more content. I felt pressured to promote the platform, to jump on social media and sell, sell, sell. There was a clear path for scale, a path for financial independence and success.

But See University had never been about making financial independence and success. In fact, creating income had been an afterthought. This project had been more about legacy. It'd been about creating a memorial to my brother. As the project grew, though, the legacy aspect was rapidly giving way to platform growth and success.

What was more, I was beginning to grow weary of photography. It had begun to feel like a glass of water. I could see into it, even through it. And that translucence made it feel like there was nothing more for me to understand about it. I started to suspect that if I continued to pour myself into See University, producing more and more photography lessons or even life lessons that touched on photography, I'd eventually lose my love for the art altogether. So despite the fact that See University was firing on all cylinders and more than paying the bills, I decided to step away from producing more content for it. (You can still access See University classes today at seeuniversity.com.)

Once I stepped away, a sort of clarity set in. I realized why my passion for photography was starting to run dry, and it wasn't just about being burned-out over making videos. Over the past few years, I'd been using my photography work and my desire to leave a legacy as a safety net or maybe an excuse.

I was using it to avoid my most compelling but most daunting idea: The Purpose Hotel.

Where photography was a glass of water, The Purpose Hotel was an ocean. Where photography had little appeal left, The Purpose Hotel was intriguing. Where I'd exhausted the depths of photographic knowledge—or felt I had—The Purpose Hotel had unknown depths to explore. It was mysterious, frightening, and thrilling. And where See University provided an opportunity to leave a certain legacy—one with my name on it—The Purpose Hotel provided an opportunity to leave a legacy with broader implications.

I wasn't quite ready to go all in on that idea just yet. But something was shifting.

One of the hardest lessons to learn in life is when to let something go, even if it's a success by the world's standards. What is success, anyhow? An idea might take shape, might make a name for you and open doors, might load you up with cash and accolades, awards, or honors. But if working with that idea doesn't fill you up, if it doesn't inspire you, if it doesn't advance its original artistic vision, it might be time to let it go. If a good idea keeps you from exploring the best idea, you have to let that one go too. Snuff it out. Blow it up. Lay it to rest, or hand it over to someone who will do something with it.

And once you do that, replace your good idea with the best idea, the most thrilling idea, even if it seems daunting.

Replace it with the idea that's so big you can't help but follow it.

LIFE IS ABOUT MORE THAN SUCCESS. IT'S ABOUT LEAVING A LEGACY OF LEARNING.

Chapter 16

THE PURPOSE HOTEL

If you want to go fast, go alone. If you want to go far, go together.

—ANONYMOUS

In the wake of See University, I sized up The Purpose Hotel idea. It still seemed too big for me, a dream of Mount Everest–size proportions. It would be the place where entrepreneurship, design, community, and humanitarianism intersected, and I had no idea where to start making it a reality. I knew this, though: possibility had become my new medium, the motif of all my work. And God used a series of seemingly disconnected events to push me into possibility.

Event one: the impromptu speech.

A couple of weeks after the idea for The Purpose Hotel dropped into my head at the Standard, I was visiting Santa Barbara for Donald Miller's Storyline conference. It was one of my favorite conferences, one that encouraged people to use their creative freedom to live a meaningful story and make an impact, and it was always such a life-giving space. Don had asked whether I'd come speak, and I'd agreed. After the presentation, I stepped onto the stage for a short question-and-answer session, but instead of taking questions, I went off script and launched into an impromptu presentation.

"I've traveled the world for the past decade as a photographer," I blurted out, "and every time I stay at a hotel, I can't help but think—what if everything here was connected to a cause or a need? What if everything here served a human in another part of the world?"

Jeremy, what are you doing?

My fingers trembled. My legs wobbled—visibly. But I kept on. "Staying one night in a hotel of purpose could impact a hundred lives or more. It could change lives and become a defining mark of this generation."

I felt a tear slide down my cheek.

Oh my gosh, don't cry.

That one tear turned into a complete emotional breakdown as I continued to share through the sort of crying that included snorts.

This is crazy. You're crazy.

"The Purpose Hotel can be a junction where community, justice, microenterprise, technology, art, and design intersect."

What had come over me? I finished my impromptu speech about the hotel and walked offstage, emotionally depleted and wondering how the crowd would take it.

I was completely unprepared for what happened next.

Folks in the room surrounded me and asked where the hotel would be and when they'd be able to book a room. They asked whether I'd chosen partnering organizations, whether they could get involved. They asked whether I'd franchise the idea. It was an overwhelmingly positive response; I never wanted to leave. And though I'd tuck the idea away for another three years, that moment fixed the dream deep in my imagination.

Event two: the dinner-date encouragement.

A few years after my impromptu conference speech, Shannon and I were at dinner with our dear friends David and Anna Zach and new friends Michael and Tsianina Lohmann. While we were waiting for appetizers, Michael talked about his fascinating career. Photography, real estate, TV and movie direction and production, selling technology patents—he'd done it all. David and I asked him questions, picked his brain. He asked us questions. We shared ideas. And as we riffed over dinner and drinks, I found myself launching into my biggest idea—you guessed it, The Purpose Hotel.

Without a moment of hesitation, Michael said, "You should do that."

But I'm not even through my full pitch yet.

"I'll do whatever I can to help you make it happen," he said. "It's a great idea."

Wait—what?

This remarkable man, who had made incredible ideas happen on a massive scale, was willing to help me? Even before I pulled together a pitch deck?

Maybe there really is something here.

Event three: the dreams embodied by a skyline.

A week or two after that dinner-date encouragement, I flew to New York for a photo shoot. Approaching the edge of the city, I looked out the window and stared at the skyline. It was a sea of buildings, hundreds if not thousands of skyscrapers. Tall, compact, majestic, understated. Concrete, glass, stone, brick. Old, new, traditional, modern. Each building had a story. Each story began with a vision. Each vision was born from a dream. And each dream grew out of an idea.

Why can't my idea turn into one of those stories?

By the time the plane landed, I'd made up my mind. After three years of lying awake at night thinking about it, cataloging ideas, and discussing it with trusted friends, the time had come.

The Purpose Hotel *was* my story.

From the airport I made two phone calls. I called Shannon first and told her it was time to move forward with the hotel. I could almost hear her smiling through the phone. We hung up, and I called Michael, but not the Michael from dinner. The other Michael, the Michael who'd been my silent business partner for years.

Event four: Michael's yes.

Michael Moore had been my business manager for more than thirteen years. He'd been the organizational brains behind every project and my partner in most of them. He'd been the sole reason I'd been able to capitalize on any of my ideas, though he'd never asked to be in the spotlight, never asked to be recognized. And over the years, I had come to understand that he knew something about almost everything.

Contracts? Yes.

Legal issues? Sure.

Accounting? Absolutely.

How to set up a nonprofit? Yup.

How to keep me on track when I've taken up permanent residence in Jeremyland? Well, if anyone could do that, Michael could.

Michael had known about The Purpose Hotel from the beginning. Other than Shannon, he was the only one I'd discussed it with on a regular basis. So when I called him that day from LaGuardia to tell him I'd finally decided to jump off the cliff, I sensed equal parts relief and hesitation.

"I'm not sure how we'll pull this off," he said. "Let's talk when you get home."

After my photo shoot, I arrived back in Nashville and drove straight to Michael's office. It was time to make the hard sale. I stormed in and said, "You have to partner with me in making this happen."

He didn't say anything.

"Neither of us have any idea what we're doing, but we can figure it out."

Still he didn't answer.

"Don't make me sell you," I said.

That's when I noticed he was on a phone call.

"I'll wait," I said as I took a seat on the other side of his desk.

By the end of the day, Michael had given me his unequivocal yes, and together we dove into the project. We spent the next few months dreaming, brainstorming, scheduling meetings with experts in the hospitality industry, identifying potential nonprofit partners, and exploring land options. Time and time again, though, we circled back to one obstacle: money. Without money the hotel was nothing more than a good idea.

We crunched numbers based on different scenarios. Location.

Size. Design. Each decision impacted the cost of the project. But no matter the scenario, we'd still need to come up with an astronomical amount of funding. And where would that funding come from?

I wish the hotel could be funded by everyday dreamers on the merit of idea alone.

How can we make it so a lot of people can give a little—a ton of people to help a ton of people?

"What about crowdfunding?" I asked Michael over acai bowls at Franklin Juice Company, the site of our triweekly breakfast meeting.

He looked up from his laptop.

I pitched the idea harder. The hotel had always been about people helping people, I said. Didn't it make sense to invite fellow dreamers into this story from the very beginning?

"I had a friend do a Kickstarter for a camera bag he wanted to create," I told Michael. "He needed $100,000 and ended up raising $5 million. Surely if he could raise millions for a bag, we could raise a couple of million for the hotel."

Event five: the failed Kickstarter.

Michael agreed, and we started working on the first Kickstarter campaign for The Purpose Hotel that very night. We pulled together the materials we'd need to make a compelling presentation—the dream, budgetary needs, designs, 3-D renderings. We dialed in The Purpose Hotel message and identified the ways the hotel would contribute the most social good to the largest number of marginalized people. We outlined our pitch and then threw our efforts into the production of a campaign video with our friends at Cliff Co., a media company that bills itself as an "impact storytelling agency." We knew they could nail the presentation, and they did. A few months later, in the summer of 2016, we launched the Kickstarter campaign with a two-million-dollar fund-raising goal and invited the world to join us in our dream for the world's first Purpose Hotel.

I leveraged my entire network, all my friends, every connection I had. I hustled as much media coverage as I could get, both in print and online. I did interviews promoting the Kickstarter, hoping it would blow up. We caught the attention of *Rolling Stone, Forbes, Huffington Post, Condé Nast Traveler,* and even the United Nations, all of which led to backing by thousands of dreamers.

Pledges rolled in. Thousands of pledges. Some people pledged one dollar, some a hundred dollars, some ten thousand dollars. People were hungry for change in the hospitality sector, and our little campaign was proving it.

On the day the campaign ended, we had reached a grand total of $750,000, a tremendously impressive amount of money. We'd fallen short of our goal, though, and because Kickstarter is an all-or-nothing crowdfunding platform, we didn't receive a dime. As well as we did, as much money that was pledged, as many people who offered support, as positive the press that we garnered, it wasn't enough. We'd failed, and as a result of that failure, The Purpose Hotel didn't have two nickels to rub together.

I knew this wasn't the end though. Something in my gut told me we could make this work, and if I'd learned anything, it was to trust my gut. We went back to the drawing board, ran the numbers again and again. We reviewed our work, our business models, our branding, our architecture, our plan.

Michael was the first to see where we'd gone wrong. Maybe we'd been too ambitious, he said. Maybe we didn't need quite so much money to get this thing off the ground. Maybe two million dollars was too lofty a goal. If we were able to raise a few hundred thousand dollars, that would buy us the time we needed to stay in the game until we could attract additional investors.

Event six: the successful Kickstarter campaign.

Following Michael's coolheaded calculations, we set a smaller goal—$347,000—and relaunched the campaign. Six weeks later, after reaching back out to the generous souls who'd pledged the first time around and utilizing the connections we'd made through the positive campaign, we more than doubled that goal. (See? Failure is only failure if you don't learn the lessons, if you let it keep you down.)

We'd followed our instincts, risked failure a second time. But this time our instincts were proven right, and now we had enough cash to lay the foundation for the hotel.

With the successful Kickstarter campaign under our belt, I could feel the winds shifting. There were still hurdles to clear, but the support and the encouragement were beginning to dwarf the doubt, the disbelief, the fear. There was new strength setting in, too, the strength that comes from believing you can do all things through Christ who strengthens you, through Christ who gives you dreams.

Event seven: the nightmare before Christmas.

So many things were coming together—more than a handful of events, to be sure—and so much of it seemed like the fruit of our efforts, our dreams. But as if to show that all dreams are subject to a little divine whimsy, God decided to intervene with a little miracle of His own.

My earliest vision of The Purpose Hotel was big. Flagship big.

Big building. Expansive lobby. Hundreds of rooms. A large presence in Nashville, with franchise locations in every major city in the United States, maybe the world. It was a pretty particular vision for a photographer with no experience in the hotel industry, no properties under management, and no way to finance the idea. My dreams have always been oversized, I suppose.

After the Kickstarter, momentum and publicity on our side, Michael and I set out to find the perfect piece of real estate, the most important decision of any hotel project. We scouted locations around downtown Nashville, but the real estate for sale was either too small, too expensive, or improperly zoned. So we expanded our search and looked at property outside the heart of the city. And finally, after a year, we settled for a less-than-optimal location. It was a parcel in a hip part of town, an area that had urban potential. It was surrounded by stylish bars, trendy restaurants, and shops galore. The walkable business district had charming architecture, was home to a historic park, and hosted a weekly farmers market. It wouldn't allow us to build the massive hotel I had envisioned though. We'd have to settle for more of a boutique hotel, one with just over one hundred rooms.

Okay, so we'll start small.

Maybe down the road, we can grow it and scale it up to something bigger.

Our elation over finding the perfect place was short-lived though. Six months into negotiations, everything fell apart. The chair of the neighborhood board called and asked whether I could meet him at a local coffee shop. I was under the gun, making last-minute preparations for the next day's Help-Portrait event. But the request sounded important, so I texted my response, telling him I was on my way. Within minutes I was walking into the coffee shop, and I could sense the weight before he said a word.

He'd been excited about my idea. A hotel like that would surely impact thousands of lives, he'd said.

"But," he said, "the neighborhood has development fatigue, and the board felt they needed to put a moratorium on new development."

And just like that, the deal was dead.

Six months of work down the drain.

Have we come this far to fail?

I need a little hope here, God.

I need a Christmas miracle.

Dejection, failure, depression—I swam in it all night, barely slept a wink. The next morning, as I loaded up the car for our ninth annual Help-Portrait event, Shannon stood outside with me, trying her best to cheer me up. Things would turn around, she said. I wasn't so sure. It seemed as if there were too many obstacles.

Event eight: the Christmas miracle.

I was the first to the church where Help-Portrait would take place, and I did my best to choke back my disappointment as I set up the lighting. I was so deep into my feelings, I didn't even hear Santa Claus enter the room. Santa—or Robert, as his friends and family called him—was a regular volunteer at Help-Portrait, but I didn't know much about him except his name, the fact that he grew his white beard out for six months just so he could look the part of Father Christmas, and the undeniable truth that he was a hit with the kids and adults alike.

"Hey," he said now, "I heard you're building something special."

Straight to the heart.

"Yeah, I'm trying to," I said, focusing all of my attention on the knob on my softbox stand and trying not to break down.

Jeremy, don't be rude. It's not Santa's fault that your dream was shattered last night.

I could have pulled him into my pity party, could have spilled my most recent disappointment, but I didn't. Instead, I shared the vision of The Purpose Hotel, its mission to change the world through hospitality.

"Have you found a location?"

I smiled. "Not really." I told him briefly about our near miss.

"Ever thought about something closer to downtown?"

Tell me more.

"I ask because my brother and I have owned four acres next to the new convention center since 1974. We're looking for something creative that gives back, something that's really different than everything else going on."

Is this a joke?

I couldn't believe my ears, so I asked him to repeat what he'd just said.

He did, and then he asked, "Do you think you'd be interested in building your hotel on it?"

All I could do was nod and hope he knew that meant yes. A few minutes passed, and when I finally gathered myself, I told him I'd love to keep talking. And during breaks that day, we did just that.

I tried to poke holes in the plan, sure I'd find some nonstarter. Surely he'd want too much money, or the zoning would be an issue, or the land would be situated over a toxic waste dump.

"Is the land being used right now?" I asked.

"Yes, it's leased to a used-car dealer, but on a month-to-month basis."

"It's probably in the floodplain, right?" I asked, assuming the natural hazards disclosure statement would show it was in the worst possible location, a location that would make approval for construction impossible.

"Nope. It's located nowhere near it."

"Is the lot on a steep hill?" I asked.

"No, it's level and already graded."

"What are the height restrictions in the zone?" I asked, praying he didn't say forty feet.

"There aren't any."

Oh my gosh. No holes. No red flags.

We arranged a meeting the following week with Michael and Robert's brother. Michael and I took the scenic route through Music Row to get there, driving right through the most historic part of Nashville. We passed record label offices, radio stations, Owen Bradley Park, the roundabout, Vanderbilt University. I approached the civic center and looked up at the upscale hotels surrounding it—the Westin, the Omni. I looked out the window in awe of my city, wondering what it'd be like to have the first Purpose Hotel in the heart of this area.

I pulled up behind Robert's parked car just outside the used-car lot. Emerging from my car, I turned to face the dealership and scanned the enormous corner lot. "There she is," Robert said.

I was speechless. The lot was in the perfect location, it was bigger than I'd imagined, and it was just across the street from the Nashville Rescue Mission, a homeless shelter that was a potential partner in the hotel.

I retreated into Jeremyland, erased the used cars from the landscape, demolished the building, then opened up a new layer. I dropped a full-sized rendering of the hotel onto the lot. I saw its clean, abstract lines, its angled glass exterior, and the flood of people going in and out, some crossing the street and heading into the Music City Center, others turning and walking toward the Ryman Auditorium.

This is it!

And then, as I emerged from Jeremyland and came back into the moment, I remembered. The music studio where my brothers and I had recorded backup vocals as kids was only a couple of blocks away. I'd come full circle, right back to the place of my earliest childhood dreams.

This was the place for the hotel. It couldn't be more perfect. Perfect size. Perfect location. It was almost too perfect.

It was almost God-shaped.

It would take us more than a year to negotiate terms, complete due diligence, and ink a contract on that property. (Real estate deals take more time than I ever would have imagined.) In that year, however, I was never worried the deal would fall apart. My conversation with Robert about the hotel had been so genuine, so serendipitous, so *random* that I knew God had His hand in it. And if God has His hand in something, He'll work out the plan.

But it wasn't just the encounter with Robert that gave me so much hope. As I traced a line back through Robert, through the Kickstarter campaigns, through Michael's yes, through the Storyline conference, and all the way back to the idea at the Standard hotel, I could see how God had been nudging me all along. In fact, I could see how everything in my life had been a nudge in this direction. Creativity had led to design, which had led to photography, which had led to Help-Portrait, which had ultimately led to this seemingly random meeting with Robert.

How could I take credit for any of it, really? I simply followed the nudges, followed idea to idea, pushed through the fear. And now I was standing in the middle of a holy possibility.

I can see now how the biggest dreams are the sum of a hundred smaller dreams. I see how every holy possibility is the culmination of so many little decisions.

In that way, I guess you could say that dreams and possibilities are the products of faithfulness.

Faithfulness to ideas? Yes.

To execution? Yes.

To audacity and connection and service? Yes, yes, yes.

Ultimately, though, the fulfillment of dreams and possibilities comes from faithfully following the nudges of God.

And as I have continued to walk in that kind of faithfulness, as Shannon and Michael and Robert and the Purpose partners and all the others continue to walk in that faithfulness along with me, we've been able to see miraculous things happen. We've seen the hand of God at work.

You can see it too. If you'll follow the nudges of God, if you'll walk in faithfulness to the dreams He's planted in you, you'll see amazing things happen. How do I know? Because all things are possible through Christ. All you have to do is walk into those possibilities one idea at a time, one decision at a time.

Faithfully.

THE FULFILLMENT
OF DREAMS AND
POSSIBILITIES
COMES FROM
FAITHFULLY
FOLLOWING
THE NUDGES
OF GOD.

Chapter 17

THE ART OF DREAMING

> One resists the invasion of armies; one does
> not resist the invasion of ideas.
>
> **–ATTRIBUTED TO VICTOR HUGO**

We can't give ground to fear, can't let it stop us or limit our possibilities. I didn't, even though I never quite knew how those possibilities would turn out. And even now I still don't know how the saga of The Purpose Hotel will end. I don't know whether it'll be a huge success or a colossal failure.

As of the writing of this book, we haven't broken ground on the hotel, but the dream is shaping up. The architectural concepts are complete. Investors are backing the cause, and financing is coming together to build this new concept, this influential hotel chain. We're exploring permitting and land-use regulations. We're looking forward to the day when the construction hardware moves onto the lot. We've found incredible partners to manage the hotel.

There's no turning back now. And though that could cause a lot of anxiety, a lot of fear, I trust the vision. I trust the supporters. I trust the thousands of hours put into this hotel by our team. What was once my idea has become a community dream, and together we're walking into it. See the power of ideas?

There was a time in my life when I didn't appreciate how fragile ideas really were. I didn't realize that "I can'ts" and "I shouldn'ts" and "I'm afraids" can hijack a grander scheme, a larger purpose.

Thankfully, God brought me through most of those can'ts and shouldn'ts and fears. Thankfully, He taught me to overcome setbacks and failure and to move into big ideas with good people. He taught me to shoot big, to break the right rules, to dream audaciously, and to collaborate with others to bring extraordinary dreams to life. Through it all, He's shown what He can do with an average-intelligence kid who's crazy enough to believe that all things are possible.

People still ask me, "What if it all falls apart?" and "Aren't you afraid it'll be a colossal public failure?" and "Is it wise to give up your photography career for . . . *this*?" I respond the same way each time: true failure is allowing fear to keep you from trying; fear is the enemy of possibility. And if they have the time, if they're willing to listen, I share how fear could have disrupted so many of my dreams, my possibilities, along the way.

What if I had allowed my fear of technology to keep me from learning Photoshop? Would I have started down the career path of design?

What if fear had kept me from walking over and talking with Shannon? Would I be married to a woman who has encouraged me to chase down the best ideas, follow the best dreams? I certainly wouldn't be the father to the best kids, to Adler, Eisley, Ebbe, and Eli.

What if fear had kept me from starting Pixelgrazer? Would I have ever picked up a camera again?

And what if fear had prevented me from jumping into photography in the first place? Would I have ever landed at the Standard hotel in Los Angeles?

What if? What if? What if?

Our lives bend around our answers to the what-ifs. Our lifelines shift with each decision we make. So shouldn't we make each decision with God-sized possibilities in mind? I think so. In fact, I think it's the only way we'll make this world a better place.

These days I like to close my eyes and relive my story. When I do, I end up in the same future every time—the opening of The Purpose Hotel. This is the God-sized possibility that is driving me at this point in my life.

I imagine myself walking through the front doors of the hotel and into a spacious lobby. The last rays of sun stream through the glass-paneled walls. I follow the sound of running water to the center of the lobby, where a fountain bubbles up. Beside the fountain is a spigot so travelers can fill their water bottles. Both the fountain and the spigot are provided by charity: water, an organization dedicated to bringing clean water to those in need.

In the lobby, three women sit on colorful couches and chairs covered in hand-dyed fabrics from around the world. I see the sleek lines of the furniture in my imagination, low and modern.

The colors are bright, clean, simple, like you might see in a modern home décor magazine. There is a sense of celebration as those three women share coffee and laugh. Above them, a "purpose tracker" shows the real-time impact of the hotel. This many children sponsored. This many water wells dug. This much money given to fight against human trafficking. I imagine the numbers ticking upward, a sign of lives being changed.

At the front desk, I check in with a woman wearing a name tag: "Hello! My Name Is Roz." She smiles, welcomes me, hands me a key card. Turning the key card over, I notice the story of the Giving Keys, a jewelry company that shares its profits with the transitional homeless of Los Angeles.

Leaving the desk, I walk to the elevator. Passing a donation bin, I read, "Donate one item from your suitcase to give to the homeless." Above it, I notice the painting of an enormous face on a giant canvas, the creation of a local artist. On the opposite wall hangs a collage of prints by Canadian photographer Joey L.—photos of a Native American woman from New Mexico; a group of indigenous farmers in the field, laughing; a little girl running through the streets of some European city—each piece a celebration of the art of human connection.

I exit the elevator and make my way to my dream room. On the door is a monitor, and it shows the name and face of a child in need. Under the name runs a snippet of her story, how proceeds from that night's stay will help provide her with food, clothing, and education. I smile knowing a portion of my room fee will go to sponsor her family.

The television plays as I enter the room, the story of The Purpose Hotel running.

The water by your bed is provided by this water-well-digging NGO.

The snacks in the minibar are certified fair-trade products and provided by this nonprofit.

The linens on your bed are provided by this group of artisans in Southeast Asia.

The furniture in the room is made by an organization that teaches ex-cons marketable skills so they can reintegrate into society.

When you order room service, a portion of the proceeds will go to a nonprofit working to bring food security to impoverished communities across the globe.

Check out the materials by your bed to read more about our Purpose Hotel partners and how you can join them in the work.

I can almost see the expressions of those affected by the hotel, the television cutting to their faces. A local man from Nashville, once homeless and unemployed, now works in the maintenance department. A child in Haiti smiles as she shares her dream of being a doctor. A mother in Africa holds up some of the hand-dyed fabrics that are used throughout the hotel. Their stories are the centerpiece of the hotel's story.

I set my bags down in my imagined hotel room, open my computer to connect to the Wi-Fi. A pop-up banner asks me whether I'd like to connect to the free Wi-Fi or upgrade for a small fee. A percentage of the upgrade fee will go to help finance efforts to end sex trafficking, the banner says. I spring for the upgrade, and I'm taken to a web page where a former sex worker shares her story of freedom.

I send a few e-mails, check the news, then close my computer. I go to the restroom to freshen up before bed, notice the soap from Thistle Farms. A sticker on the back of the soap wrapper reads,

"Thistle Farms offers women hope and healing through a holistic residential program, employment with one of our social enterprises, and a growing national and global network dedicated to changing a culture that allows human beings to be bought and sold."

I go back to the bedroom, turn down the sheets, and turn off the bedside lamp. I stare at the ceiling, the stories of the hotel mingling in my head and coming together in what will surely form the tapestry of my dreams. I close my eyes, and I can hear my parents' voices echoing.

You can do all things . . .

We're years away from this dream becoming a reality, but I don't doubt that it will, not even for a moment. And in this in-between time, this liminal space between possibility and reality, I consider all the people connected to the hotel. Shannon. Our family. Michael. My parents and brothers. The Storyline encouragers, the financial supporters. The designers, architects, construction crews. The partners, investors, and bankers. The management company. Future guests. Greeters and maître d's. Baristas and bartenders. Chefs and servers. Maintenance folks. Cleaning staff. You.

All of us are in this thing called life together. We each carry our own hopes, dreams, and fears, but we each carry worlds of possibility too. If we let them, those possibilities can change the world.

"You can do all things through Christ who strengthens you," my parents always said. Thankfully, I was just simple enough to believe it. And that has made all the difference.

YOU CAN DO
ALL THINGS
THROUGH
CHRIST WHO
STRENGTHENS
YOU.

ACKNOWLEDGMENTS

God, thank You for a lifetime of paper wads. Because of You, through You, and thanks to You, I'm possible.

To my wife, Shannon—You're my best friend forever. Thanks for listening to twenty years of crazy ideas and knowing how to filter out the bad ones (the vast majority) and when to say yes to the few good ones. Who knows how many dead-end roads I would have gone down without you.

To my whole crew—Shannon, Adler, Eisley, Eli, and Ebbe—I love you all so much. It's a good thing these are written words, because if this were audio or video, we all know I'd be just a big bucket of tears. My soul aches when I'm away from you. Home is wherever you are.

Mom and Dad (Mike and Esther Cowart)—I love you. Thank you for seeing beyond what I could see and encouraging me in ways I never knew I needed. I'm a better person and parent because of you.

To Mike and Benji, my older brothers—You are my original heroes, and I love you so much and am so proud of you both. Mike, Benji and I can't wait to make more music with you in heaven one day. We miss you daily.

To my extended family—Noah, Reese, Braden, Kyndall, Zac, Maisy, Jenna, Penny, Aggie, John, Griffin, Nancy, Sam, Cindy, Pat—I love you all so much, and I can't wait for a lifetime more of memory making with all of you.

To my old Hendersonville community—You all helped shape me and made me who I am today. Thank you.

To my business partner, Michael Moore—I might be picking the mountains to climb, but you're pulling me the entire way up. I don't know how you do it. Forever grateful.

To the rest of the Treeline Bamboo team—David, Matt, Cindy, Mimy, Chris, Brandon—I'm so grateful for your expertise and support in everything I do.

Kyle Chowning—You've been a rock in my life ever since I met you. So much of what I've done wouldn't have happened without your wisdom and friendship.

Jimmy Abegg—Thanks for telling me to quit my job and then telling me to start shooting back in the day. You changed my course forever.

Jeremy Pinnix—I love that we've woven in and out of each other's lives for twenty-plus years now, yet the friendship has always remained steadfast. You are a genius, and I'm so lucky to get to work with you.

To my former agent, Caryn Weiss—I owe so much to you. We had quite a run together, and I'll never forget it. Thank you for taking a chance on me.

To Andres Martinez and all past photoshoot assistants—Dres, you're truly the younger brother I never had. Love you, dude. To the rest of my crews over the years—Thank you for working so hard on my behalf. Without you, the magic wouldn't happen. I so appreciate your hustle.

To David Zach, Marshall Lee, Matt Lehman, Lee Steffen, Jon

Acuff, Carlos Whittaker, Derek Webb, Gabe Lyons, Micah Kandros, Dave Barnes, Jeff Huxford, Steven Bailey, Brad Henderson, Jamie George, Darren Whitehead, Joel Edwards, Curtis Zackery, David Bean, Austin Mann, Spencer Combs—Y'all are my dudes. You are the "great minds share ideas" friends I get to share this creative journey with.

To the Zachs, the Lees, the Chownings, the Cashs, the Huxfords, and our entire missional community group—We love doing this life thing with you all.

To Gabe Lyons, Dave Blanchard, and the entire Axiom, Q, and Praxis communities—It's tough to find words, but thanks for always pointing me to true north.

To Esther Fedorkevich and the Fedd Agency—Thank you for believing in me enough to reach out. This book is real because of you.

The entire team at HarperCollins—Thank you for showing me the ropes and doing such an incredible job. You have made this so fun and painless.

To Seth Haines—This book may be called *I'm Possible*, but that doesn't apply to writing for me, sadly. Thank you for helping me find the words when I (really) can't.

To the online community—The Help-Portrait participants around the world, The Purpose Hotel Kickstarter backers, the See University members, the audiences I've spoken to around the country, and my online followers—Thank you. I'm tearing up a little as I write this one. Y'all are such a gift of encouragement. You have no idea.

To the growing Purpose Hotel team—Michael Moore, Kim Lewis, Jeremy Pinnix, Matt Lehman, WP, Hastings, and all future team members and employees—Buckle up. This is going to be a blast.

To Saoirse—This book is dedicated to you because you're possible. Keep fighting, friend. You're an inspiration.

ABOUT THE AUTHOR

Named the "Most Influential Photographer on the Internet" by *Huffington Post* in 2014, JEREMY COWART is an award-winning photographer, artist, and entrepreneur whose goal in life is to use his creative platform to inspire and help others. Jeremy is a sought-after speaker, having presented at TEDx, the United Nations, and creative conferences across the country. His latest endeavor is The Purpose Hotel, a planned global for-profit hotel chain designed to fuel the work of not-for-profit organizations. He's also the founder of a global photography movement, Help-Portrait, and an online teaching platform, SeeUniversity.com. He lives in Franklin, Tennessee, with his wife and four children.

For more, visit
JeremyCowart.com
@jeremycowart